THE TRAGEDIES OF SOPHOCLES

Intended for the general reader and students with or without Greek, this book sets separate discussions of Sophocles' seven plays between an essay that outlines modern approaches to Greek tragedy and a final chapter that spotlights a key moment in the reception of each work.

Focusing on the tragedies' dramatic power and the challenges with which they confront an audience, Morwood refuses to confine them within a supposedly Sophoclean template. They are seven unique works, only alike in the fact that they are all major masterpieces. The reception chapter deals with Milton's *Samson Agonistes*, the first Cambridge Greek play (*Ajax*), the Strauss/Hofmannsthal opera *Elektra*, Anouilh's *Antigone*, Pasolini's film *Edipo Re*, Seamus Heaney's *The Cure at Troy* (*Philoctetes*) and Martin Crimp's *Cruel and Tender* (*Women of Trachis*).

James Morwood is an Emeritus Fellow of Wadham College, Oxford. Among his numerous publications are translations of eleven plays by Euripides in the Oxford World's Classics series, *The Plays of Euripides* and an edition of Euripides' *Suppliant Women*. His interest in drama goes beyond the classical world: he has also written *The Life and Works of Richard Brinsley Sheridan* and contributed to a book on Tom Stoppard.

GREECE AND ROME LIVE

Also available in this series:
Ancient Greece in Film and Popular Culture, Gideon Nisbet (2006; second edition 2008)
Augustine: The Confessions, Gillian Clark (2005)
Gruesome Deaths and Celibate Lives: Christian Martyrs and Ascetics, Aideen M. Hartney (2005)
Hadrian's Wall and its People, Geraint Osborn (2006)
Hannibal: Rome's Greatest Enemy, Dexter Hoyos (2008)
Julius Caesar, Robert Garland (2004)
The Politics of Greek Tragedy, David M. Carter (2007)
Reading Catullus, John Godwin (2008)

Forthcoming titles:
After Virgil: The Poetry, Politics and Perversion of Roman Epic, Robert Cowan
Ancient Rome at the Cinema: Story and Spectacle in Hollywood and Rome, Elena Theodorakopoulos
Augustus: Caesar's Web: Power and Propaganda in Augustan Rome, Matthew D.H. Clark
The Classical Greek House, Janett Morgan
Greek Tyranny, Sian Lewis
The Law in Ancient Greece, Christopher Carey
Pausanias: An Ancient Guide to Greece, John Taylor
The Trojan War, Emma Stafford

THE TRAGEDIES OF SOPHOCLES

James Morwood

BRISTOL
PHOENIX
PRESS

Cover image: *Oedipus and the Sphinx*, 1808 (oil on canvas) by Jean Auguste Dominque Ingres (1780–1867) Louvre Museum, Paris (The Bridgeman Art Library).

Sigmund Freud, who made the myth of Oedipus and the Sphinx central to psychoanalysis, had in his art collection an Athenian black-figured oil or perfume flask (*c.* 490–470 BC) illustrating their story, as well as a south Italian terracotta statuette of the Sphinx (late 5th, early 4th century BC).

First published in 2008 by
Bristol Phoenix Press
an imprint of The Exeter Press
Reed Hall, Streatham Drive
Exeter, Devon EX4 4QR
UK
www.exeterpress.co.uk

British Library Cataloguing in Publication Data
A catalogue record for this book is available from the British Library

Paperback ISBN 13: 978 1 904675 72 3
Hardback ISBN 13: 978 1 904675 71 6

Typeset by Carnegie Book Production, Lancaster in Chaparral Pro 11pt on 15pt
Printed in Great Britain by CPI Antony Rowe, Chippenham

CONTENTS

A pencil jotting of the Cambridge *Ajax* by Robert Farren (see p. 84)x

AGAMEMNON. *Remember the sort of man to whom you give the favour.*
ODYSSEUS. *This man was my enemy, but he was noble once.* (lines 1354–5)

PREFACE

O nly seven of Sophocles' plays, out of a likely total of 123, survive complete and we know the production dates of just two of those, 409 BC for *Philoctetes* and 401 for the posthumous *Oedipus at Colonus*. These considerations make it dangerous not only to generalize about the plays, speculating on what may be characteristically Sophoclean in them, but also to trace any development in the playwright's art. I have discussed the tragedies in their possible but by no means certain order and I have tried to view each of them on its own terms. My only presupposition has been that a great dramatist such as Sophocles is likely to be doing very different things in all of them. Writing this book has confirmed me in that presupposition. The obvious drawback to my approach, which clearly requires that each work should be viewed in its entirety, is that it leaves the numerous fragments of other plays on the cutting room floor. This is especially regrettable in the case of the substantial fragments of the satyr play *Trackers*, one of a likely total of 25 to 30 by Sophocles in this genre, which reveals him as a notable exponent of festive comedy.[1]

I begin the book with a chapter entitled 'Taking Bearings', which outlines various ways in which critics currently tend to approach Sophocles and Greek tragedy more generally. My hope is that this will enable readers to identify which approaches they find most sympathetic or indeed to reject all of them and find their own way to the heart of the plays. I conclude with a chapter on the reception of the tragedies, dealing with one highly significant moment in the evolution of each of them in the modern world.

I have assumed a certain knowledge of the seven plays, though of course the chapters on the individual works are free-standing. If readers are completely unfamiliar with any or all of them, they would be well advised to read – or, better still, see – them before they turn to what I have to say. Helpful plot summaries can be found in Storey and Allan (2005). Footnotes have been kept to a minimum and I have tried to avoid the technical language that can obstruct understanding of Greek tragedy as much as it can illuminate it. The small number of words in this category which I *have* used are defined in the Glossary.

The few abbreviations of classical names and titles are those given in the *Oxford Classical Dictionary*, 3rd edition (1996). Shakespearean references are to *The Oxford Shakespeare*, 2nd edition (2005). 'The double time scheme in *Antigone*' appeared in *Classical Quarterly* 43 (i) (1993).

My warm thanks go to all those directors and actors, scholars, students and friends who have fostered my life-long love of this dramatist. My most immediate debts are to John Betts, Chris Collard, Eric Dugdale, Ian McAuslan, Judith Mossman, Bernard O'Donoghue and David Raeburn. I am especially grateful to Pat Easterling, who not only made available to me the album on the 1882 *Ajax* in the archive of the Cambridge Greek play in the University Library, but also generously took on the task of reading my manuscript for the Bristol Phoenix Press. Her comments were pure gold. I must, of course, couple these expressions of gratitude with the acknowledgement that I take full responsibility for the moments when my obstinacy, perversity or ignorance has led me astray.

James Morwood, January, 2008
Wadham College, Oxford
james.morwood@wadh.ox.ac.uk

CHAPTER 1

TAKING BEARINGS

In 1988 John Gould, a supremely insightful commentator on Greek tragedy, remarked on the vulnerability of *Oedipus the King* to 'multiple possibilities of misunderstanding'. Homing in on some misreadings of the play provoked by its resemblance to a detective story, he declared that they 'remind one irresistibly of Thurber's story "The Macbeth Murder Mystery"'. Gould's reference is to a story by the American humorist James Thurber, in which a devotee of crime fiction has a startlingly new take on Shakespeare's play: Macduff did it. 'Hercule Poirot would have got him easily.' While it is probably true that Sophocles has fallen victim to strange misreadings to a lesser extent than Euripides, he continues to take some hard knocks. What, for example, is one supposed to make of a 1982 editor's comment, preserved in the second edition of 2006, on Oedipus' statement to the deputation of Theban citizens supplicating him for his help in dealing with the plague? 'I know well,' says the king, 'that you are all sick and, sick as you are, there is none so sick as I am.' (*Oedipus the King* 59–61) The editor comments that Oedipus 'is supposed to be suffering from [the plague] himself, if we take line 60 at its face value'.

A similarly disconcerting response to the language of the theatre occurs when a 1973 editor, in another well-thumbed modern edition, comments on a passage in *Electra* in which the heroine pours forth an ecstatic greeting to the old Tutor, exclaiming, 'Hail, O father – for I seem to look upon my father' (1361). 'Orestes and the [Tutor],' our editor observes, 'in haste to murder Clytaemnestra, have reckoned without Electra, who now insists on inflicting upon them a period of delay during which she develops her illusion that the [Tutor] is in fact her father walking! The interlude is a curious one.' As Alice remarked, curiouser and curiouser!

If some approaches have closed rather than opened doors into these great plays, we need to investigate what useful avenues are available to us. Without in any way wishing to claim that the following paths are the 'right' – or indeed the only – ones, I propose to discuss some of the directions that current criticism has taken. For those who wish to set these approaches within a broader historical context, I recommend Simon Goldhill's essay, 'Modern critical approaches to Greek tragedy' (Easterling, 1997a).

Much of the terrain for the modern debate was mapped out as long as a century ago by Gilbert Murray, Regius Professor of Greek at Oxford, editor of the first Oxford Classical Texts of Aeschylus and Euripides, man of the theatre and highly successful popularizer of all things Greek. It was he who insisted on the political nature of the plays, their historical resonances, their social urgency, the religious and anthropological assumptions that permeate them and the remarkable psychological truth in their delineation of character (Murray, 2005).

The last feature will be discussed later in this essay and in the chapters on the individual plays. Let us first examine the others, beginning with politics. In a famous essay dating from 1987, Simon Goldhill argued that the civic ceremonies with which the festival of the Dionysia began – libations poured quite possibly by the ten generals, the presentation of tribute by the cities in the Athenian empire, a parade of war orphans – inevitably set the plays that followed in a political, Athenian – and therefore democratic – framework. Goldhill suggested that 'the tragic texts seem to question, examine, and often subvert the language of the city's order'. When Goldhill's essay first appeared, it brought with it the whiff of grapeshot but, from the perspective of twenty years on, it seems decidedly odd that it gave rise to a maelstrom of *odium academicum*. After all, if it is objected that many parts of the plays do not seem to be imbued with politics, it is worth pointing out, as I have done elsewhere (Morwood, 2002), that 'Shakespeare's greatest play about love, *Antony and Cleopatra*, could with equally good reason be called his greatest play about politics; that Beaumarchais' wonderful comedy about the workings of the human heart, *The Marriage of Figaro*, first performed in Paris in 1784, is a blazing revolutionary manifesto; and that the entire oeuvre of Chekhov lays bare the reasons why the society it portrays would inevitably be swept aside in 1917'. Sophocles' *Electra* is a play of revenge conducted within a dysfunctional family. In that sense it is domestic. However, it matters profoundly that this is not just *any* family but a royal one. A king has been murdered. A usurper has married his queen, sits on his throne and displaces the legitimate children with offspring of his own (589–90). We are not in the squalid domestic world of, say, Shostakovitch's *Lady Macbeth of Mtsensk*. Big political issues are at stake.

That said, the debate initiated by Goldhill has naturally moved on since 1987. In an article dating from 2000, Richard Seaford listed 'but a few' of the 'practices of the Athenian polis [city] that … cannot be ignored by serious interpreters of tragedy', citing democracy, philosophy, written law, the mysteries, the development of rhetoric, the legal position of women, the Peloponnesian war and hero-cult. No doubt he would happily add the family to his list. There is a problem, however. If the definition of what the word political means has to be widened to this extent, one is tempted to wonder just how useful it is as a label. Then in 2003, P.J. Rhodes challenged the democratic Athenocentricity of Goldhill's position, arguing that, while the institutional setting of the plays 'inevitably took a particular form in democratic Athens, that was an Athenian version of institutions found more generally in the Greek world, and even in the Athenian version many features do not seem distinctly democratic ... Themes have often been said to be democratic which are better seen as concerns of *polis*-dwelling Greeks in general.' Clearly there is quite a lot of mileage left in this field.

On the subject of the historical resonances of Greek tragedy, attempts to light upon particular Athenian politicians as models for Sophoclean characters have (fortunately in my view) failed to get us very far, possibly because of the uncertainty of the dates of most of the plays and the subsequent problems in relating their dramatis personae to specific political figures. However, Bernard Knox's argument that Oedipus the King 'is a dramatic embodiment of the creative vigour and intellectual daring of the fifth-century spirit' (Knox, 1984) is a brilliant exemplar of the historical approach. For other valuable work in this area, see Sommerstein *et al.* (1993) and Pelling (1997).

If I may be permitted to focus on a single area to illustrate social approaches to Greek tragedy, I should like to discuss attitudes to its treatment of women. The most influential recent book in this area is Laura McClure's *Spoken Like a A Woman* (1999), in which she declares that her purpose is 'not to recover actual women's voices, or to suggest an exact correspondence between historical women and their literary depiction, but to understand how women's voices were conceptualised by male-authored texts produced both in Athens and elsewhere over a broad span of time'. Unfortunately McClure's book is largely a Sophocles-free zone but its strategies can of course be adopted with our playwright. A parallel area of research was launched by Judith Mossman (2001). In an all too short (and again Sophocles-free) article, she put the question laid aside by McClure, 'Did the Greek tragedians try to make their women sound like women?' It is very much to be hoped that this line of investigation will be pursued. One stimulating discussion of women in tragedy which *does* include Sophocles must definitely be mentioned, Helene Foley's *Female Acts in Greek Tragedy* (2001). And I should perhaps end with Christiane Sourvinou-Inwood's caveat against importing the assumptions of modern feminism into discussion of ancient drama. She warns against readings 'which deploy by default the culturally determined filters of modern gender discourse'.

Sourvinou-Inwood's 2003 book from which I quote deals primarily with religion, the subject to which I now turn, and, like McClure's on women's voices, proves disappointingly reticent about the treatment of the gods that we encounter specifically in Sophocles. Her contention, summed up in her discussion of Euripides' *Hippolytus*, that 'tragedy presents [a] reassuring image of an ordered cosmos, policed and guaranteed by Zeus' strikes me for one as decidedly wide of the mark if applied, say, to *Women of Trachis* (see pp. 34–5). However, Sourvinou-Inwood has undeniably made an important contribution to the debate. Most scholars, though, would argue that the view of the gods that we can extrapolate from Sophocles' plays tends to the opaque. Knox (1964) called them 'the most remote and mysterious creation in all Greek literature'. Certainly we seem to see them through a glass darkly (Parker, 1999). As Gould (1996a) remarks:

Between the two worlds of gods and men there is communication, in the imagined world of Sophoclean theatre: it comes in the form of dreams, oracles, and the reading of signs by seers such as Tiresias. Men and women try to guide their decisions by their understanding of such communications. But such understanding is almost always false: the language and the signs used by divinity are everywhere ambiguous, however simple in appearance, and they are systematically and readily misunderstandable, even if they are to hand.

Indeed, play after play reveals the slippery nature of such communication. Witness the oracle in *Philoctetes*. Does it or does it not foretell that *both* Philoctetes *and* his bow will go to Troy? As Gould concludes: 'The recurring pattern of Sophoclean tragedy is that all falls into place and coheres only in retrospect: recognition after the event.'

Gould is surely correct in the matter of communication between gods and men. However, it is no doubt a mistake to generalize about Sophocles' presentation of the divine. Each play has its own agenda. There is an appalling bleakness to the song in *Oedipus the King* in which the chorus express their wish that the play's terrible oracles should be true rather than they should find their religious belief shattered (897–902 – p. 54). On the other hand, the 'happy' issues of *Philoctetes* and *Oedipus at Colonus* in my view evince a world presided over by ultimately benevolent deities. They share this territory with Shakespeare's late romances, though, as in them, the happiness is certainly qualified.

The anthropological approach can conveniently be exemplified by Vernant's essay (Vernant, 1983), which deals with *Oedipus the King*, on the Athenians' treatment of the scapegoat, discussed on p. 47. It is an approach that has paid rich dividends. The concept of the ephebe, the young man undergoing the rite of passage to adulthood, has also proved helpful in relation to Orestes in *Electra* and of course to Neoptolemus in *Philoctetes* (Winkler, 1990). Then awareness of hero-cult in ancient Greece leads to enhanced appreciation of the endings possibly of *Women of Trachis*, probably of *Ajax* and certainly of *Oedipus at Colonus*. Heracles, Ajax and Oedipus had all been heroized and were worshipped in fifth-century Attica, knowledge activated in the last tragedy most explicitly at 621–2 and quite possibly at *Ajax* 1166–7 and in the play's concluding tableau. If the audience can feel that the heroes have won their immortality and were worshipped, or at least appeased, in fifth-century Athens, a note of consolation, indeed of celebration, may be struck (Knox, 1964). For the on-going interest in ritual in tragedy, a good place to start is Easterling (1993). Robert Parker (2005) is excellent on all the issues raised in this paragraph (as well as on religion in the Greek theatre), and another valuable book is Walter Burkert's classic *Greek Religion: Archaic and Classical* (1985).

Moving on from the approaches suggested by Gilbert Murray, we come to consideration of the geography of the plays. In a highly influential article published in 1990, Froma Zeitlin suggested that the Attic dramatists used Thebes as a location dramatically 'other' than Athens itself. 'Thebes,' she argues,

> consistently supplies the radical tragic terrain where there can be no escape from the tragic in the resolution of conflict or in the institutional provision of a civic future beyond the world of the play.

Athens, in contrast, 'is the scene where theatre can and does "escape" the tragic, and where reconciliation and transformation are made possible'. There has been considerable calibration of this view, not least by Zeitlin herself, and Oliver Taplin (1999) is right to warn against 'any simple formulation of an Athens-positive / Thebes-negative polarity'. Yet the basic distinction remains a helpful and valuable one and is clearly consonant with Sophocles' presentation of a dislocated Thebes in all three of the so-called Theban plays (*Antigone, Oedipus the King, Oedipus at Colonus*) and of the ideal location of Athens in the last one. Good work on these lines has been done by Taplin (1987) on the setting of *Philoctetes* 'within a sort of mapping of the entire span of the northern Aegean' and by John Gould (1988) on the opposition of place in *Oedipus the King* 'between the *poleis* [cities] of Thebes and Corinth, and the space "outside", the mountainsides and tracks and cross-roads of Oedipus' other world'. I myself wonder whether, in his *Women of Trachis* with its terrifying welter of visceral emotions, Sophocles is making dramatic capital out of the play's setting in Trachis, the entry into Greece (Herodotus 7.176.2 and 8.4.1), a liminal place between the wild North and the civilized Hellenic world. A particularly important contribution to the debate on the figurative geography of Greek tragedy is Edith Hall's *Inventing the Barbarian* (1989).[2] She demonstrates that the ways in which playwrights defined the barbarian world tell us very little about barbarians but a great deal about the Greeks.[3] She has calibrated her insights for the new millennium in *The Theatrical Cast of Athens*, a landmark book which views Greek drama in a multiplicity of ways, breaking down the barriers between the different methodologies outlined in this chapter.

The chorus calls for a brief discussion. As usual in Greek tragedy, the characters who make up Sophocles' choruses are generally marginal within their society. In two plays, *Women of Trachis* and *Electra*, they are women. In *Ajax* and *Philoctetes* they are sailors who are utterly dependent on their captains. In the remaining three plays they are old men. With the possible exceptions of the *Oedipus the King* noblemen and the *Antigone* elders (see pp. 54 and 37–8), none of these groups can speak with any political authority,[4] though the women of Trachis are certainly capable of giving catastrophic advice (588–93). It now seems simplistic to believe that they direct the audience's responses to the dramatic action in a straightforward way, though much of the lyric interaction between chorus and characters surely suggests *possible* emotional responses. John Gould (1996b) sums up the function of the chorus thus:

> Clearly the chorus is a distinctive feature of Greek tragedy: the 'Chorus' of Shakespeare's *Henry V* or that of Anouilh's *Antigone* are something else. In the Greek tragic theatre, the presence of the chorus within the tragic fiction, their constant and essential presence (they are not an optional part of that fiction), creates

a collective, and in some sense 'communal', dimension for 'the tragic' and sets the tragic experience of an Electra apart from those of Hamlet, Othello, Macbeth, or Lear.

It is a formulation that remains persuasive.

As we now come to the matter of characterization, my first aim is to draw attention to the astonishing variety among the figures whom Sophocles has portrayed: Ajax, the megalomaniac solipsist who, with all his inflexibility, can yet entertain the idea of mutability and express it with such deep empathy; Odysseus, the archetype of noble humanity in *Ajax*, the Machiavellian villain in *Philoctetes*; Deianeira, so fragile, so insecure; Hercules, a brutish icon of pain; Antigone, a self-willed martyr whose defiant courage shines so brightly; Creon, immovable, deaf to appeals, yet suddenly cracking; Oedipus the king, the supremely confident, utterly intent seeker after truth; Electra, the loving princess whose upbringing by her murderess mother has warped her irretrievably; Philoctetes, the crippled hero, so intransigent, so full of hatred until his friends teach him to compromise; and the old Oedipus at Colonus, whose nature on the final count is defined not by anger but by love. When confronted with such a diverse gallery of superbly etched characters, one is tempted to echo Dryden's judgement on *The Canterbury Tales*, 'here is God's plenty'.

If any of my readers feel that I have gone too far in insisting on the diversity of Sophocles' characterizations, they will find themselves in good company. Succumbing to heresy, I have attempted to deconstruct the 'Sophoclean hero'. In a fine and enormously influential book Bernard Knox (1964) defined the characteristics of the figure who features in six of the seven plays, i.e. all of them apart from *Women of Trachis*:

Immovable once his decision is taken, deaf to appeals and persuasion, to reproof and threat, unterrified by physical violence, even by the ultimate violence of death itself, more stubborn as his isolation increases until he has no one to speak to but the unfeeling landscape, bitter at the disrespect and mockery the world levels at what it regards as failure, the hero prays for revenge and curses his enemies as he welcomes the death that is the predictable end of his intransigence.

This is eloquent writing. Within its own terms, it is utterly compelling. However, in my view, Knox's template of the Sophoclean hero has cast as much darkness as light. It has tended to obliterate the differences between the various characters in their varied contexts. It would be unfair to blame Knox for this. He freely admits that there is no single definition which 'can contain the variety and vitality of the six (*sic*) plays, the uniqueness and living personality of the different heroes'. Nevertheless this is the effect he has had. The differences simply get eroded in the desire to spot the resemblances. Another problem is that in plays in which the protagonist can be hard to identify, most obviously *Antigone* and *Philoctetes* (I swiftly pass over the excluded *Women of Trachis*), it becomes necessary not only to pronounce one of them the tragic hero but also to find reasons why another one isn't. More worrying still is the marginalization of *Women of Trachis*, just as much of a masterpiece as any of the other tragedies, which finds itself being dubbed un-Sophoclean. Every time I hear the word 'uncanonic' used of this great play, I reach Goering-like for my revolver. I would urge readers of this book to try to forget about this Knoxian construct until they have made their own evaluation of Sophocles' characters.

The scope of this chapter does not allow for discussion of all useful approaches to Greek tragedy. Two more, however, cry out to be included. One is the study of the way in which the plays were originally staged. The key figure in this area of scholarship is Oliver Taplin, whose 1977 book is a veritable landmark. A number of subsequent books cry out for mention: the excellent collection of written source material (Csapo and Slater, 1994); the helpful elucidation of that material – and much more – in Storey and Allan (2005); the fine assemblage of visual evidence in Green and Handley (1995); David Wiles' important book on masks (1991); and Oliver Taplin's *Greek Tragedy in Action* (1978). The last of these is the most immediately relevant for our purposes since, while it deals with matters of staging in all three of the tragic dramatists, Sophocles is represented by *Ajax*, *Oedipus the King* and *Philoctetes*. Taplin's account of the handling of the bow in the last of those plays is particularly illuminating and eloquent. Finally, in an increasingly crowded field, I draw attention to four books that really make one think about issues of staging, Scullion (1994), Rehm (2002), Ley (2007) and Dugdale (2008).

As our final destination, we reach the study of reception, i.e. the history of how works of art have been interpreted on their journey to our time. In the case of Greek tragedy, of course, it is largely concerned with post-classical stagings of the plays or versions of them. A good overview is given by Lorna Hardwick (2003). A particularly invigorating exemplar of this branch of study is *Greek Tragedy and the British Theatre 1660–1914* by Edith Hall and Fiona Macintosh (2005), which tells the story of how Greek tragedy, not only in translation but in various guises (or disguises such as the burlesque), exerted a powerful influence on the English stage throughout the period discussed. In addition, the stagings continuously reflected matters of urgent contemporary political and social concern. They mirrored and influenced public opinion. They radiated light amid the at times murky groves of academe. Whatever was going on in the England of these centuries, the Greek tragedians had a word for it.

The examination by Hall and Macintosh of the dialogue between the theatre in the modern world and classical Greek tragedy is highly illuminating. In dealing with the relationship of drama with important political and social issues, it steers clear of attempts to reconstruct actual performances in detail. Such attempts are surely doomed to failure. Richard Eyre, a former Director of the National Theatre, puts the matter splendidly as he comments on 'the transience of the theatre':

> that's certainly what attracts me – it's in the present tense, it's live, it's unreproducible. It's ephemeral: it lives on only in the memory, melting away after the event. I *like* seeing the set broken up after a last night, the costumes and props being put in store to be re-used in other shows. I *like* not being able to have retrospectives, not being able to archive productions. At best a production of a performance can only achieve immortality as a myth.

I fully agree that efforts to put together the nuts and bolts of yesteryear's productions go against the grain of the theatrical experience.

The final chapter of this book deals with a particular staging post in the reception of each of Sophocles' works. My discussion of the 1882 production of *Ajax* which launched the important series of Cambridge Greek plays that has continued, generally robustly, to this day, reflects its historical importance. Here, as elsewhere in this chapter, I have tried to avoid the danger I identified in the last paragraph. I limit myself to known facts about the Cambridge *Ajax* rather than attempting to bring it to life. Indeed, aesthetically it probably left rather a lot to be desired. Pat Easterling remarks that 'it is easy to guess that the early productions were in fact pretty wooden and amateurish' (1983 Cambridge Greek play programme). The section which juxtaposes *Oedipus at Colonus* with Milton's *Samson Agonistes* aims to illustrate Milton's symbiosis with Sophocles' tragedy about a blind old man. In the case of the other plays, by looking at recreations of them by great – or at least distinguished – creative artists, I have hoped to show that we can learn much about the way the on-going present has negotiated with the classical past and ensured that the blood in the veins of the old tragedies is endlessly renewed, that their pulse still beats. It is this continuum of vigorous dramatic life that I aim to celebrate in the concluding essays in this book.

CHAPTER 2

AJAX

ARMS AND THE MAN

When Ajax appears for the second time in Sophocles' play, he is sitting on the *ekkyklēma* (see glossary) amid cattle that he has slaughtered in the mad delusion that they were Greek generals. Just as he has mistaken animals for men, the tableau presented to us (at 348) may seem to blur the distinction between the would-be mass murderer and the animals that surround him. At 169 he was likened to a vulture, at 322 to a bellowing bull. Earlier Odysseus has been seen repeatedly as a hunting dog tracking its prey (5–6, 19–20, 31–3 and 37); at 103 Ajax calls him a fox. What, if any, the play invites us to consider, is the difference between men and beasts?

A remarkable feature of Sophocles' *Ajax* is that the Greek word for man (*anēr*) recurs again and again like a musical motto. It is used 83 times, considerably more than in any of his other plays,[5] and its frequent repetition urgently poses the question of what a man is. Are we in the world of Hamlet's celebratory, 'What a piece of work is a man!', or of his laconic tribute to his father, 'A was a man. Take him for all in all, / I shall not look upon his like again' (*Hamlet*, 2.2.305ff. and 1.2.186–7)? Or should we invoke the grim distinction which the Captain sent to murder King Lear and Cordelia makes between man and beast:

> I cannot draw a cart,

Nor eat dried oats. If it be man's work, I'll do't.
King Lear, Quarto 24.37–8

In a famous chorus in *Antigone* Sophocles explores the use and abuse of the genius of man (332–75). In his *Ajax* we find him similarly celebrating man's capacity for the good and the noble, while bleakly illustrating his propensity to evil, mean-spiritedness and self-regard.

Ajax himself is presented with an unsettling ambivalence. Enraged at the fact that the dead Achilles' arms were awarded not to him but to Odysseus, he has set out to kill the Greek chieftains. In the *Iliad*, Homer's great poem about the Trojan War and a frequent point of reference in Sophocles' play, he is portrayed as a man who instinctively supports his fellow Greeks, proving a stout defender of the Achaean wall and later of the ships (books 12 and 15) as well as the rescuer of Odysseus (11.473–88). Now in Sophocles' play, we discover that he had determined to slaughter them. There is certainly much to dislike in the Greek leaders Menelaus and Agamemnon when they appear but their indignant anger at what Ajax tried to do is fully justified. It was mad and unpardonable. And of this he shows not a glimmer of recognition. Just before his death he calls upon the Furies not to spare the whole Greek army but to glut themselves on it (843–4).

While Teucer brings the Iliadic Ajax vividly to mind in 1273–87, the Greek seer Calchas is quoted as giving a monstrously hubristic picture of the hero both before he came to Troy and on the battlefield there:

> That man, when first he set out from home, was found to be foolish when his father spoke well. For the latter said to him, 'My son, seek victory in arms, but always seek it with the help of god.' But boastfully and foolishly he answered, 'Father, with the aid of the gods even a man of no account could win the

mastery. But I am confident that even without then I shall win this fame.' So boastful was his speech. Then on a second occasion, when divine Athena was urging him on and telling him to turn his deadly hand upon his enemies, he then made a terrible and unspeakable response: 'Lady, stand near the rest of the Argives; where I stand, no enemy will ever break through.' By such words he brought upon himself the intolerable anger of the goddess since his thoughts kept no human measure. (762–77)

Here Ajax is incredibly unlike his Iliadic alter ego. In the epic he comes across as a regular guy, the only Greek apart from Patroclus who can get through to Achilles, in his case through his bluff plain-speaking (9.622–45). I find it hard go along with a common view of the play that sees the Sophoclean Ajax as a Homeric dinosaur compounded of heroic values and unable to cope in a newer (i.e. fifth-century) world. For one thing, his hubristic vaunts quoted above are borrowed from Aeschylus' portrait of one of the Seven against Thebes, the straightforwardly brutal Capaneus (*Seven against Thebes* 427–8), not from anyone in the *Iliad*, a work in which the heroes positively value divine aid. One may feel distress, even sympathy, for Ajax at the abject pass to which Athena has brought him at the start of the play but it is hard to argue that he doesn't ask for everything he gets.

And yet ... and yet ... This is a man who inspires deep loyalty in his men (349–50), affection in his wife (392–3, 491), devotion in his brother and respect and admiration in his enemy Odysseus (1336–45 and 1355–7). Once he has recovered from his madness, he shows a compellingly flinty integrity, an ultimate refusal to compromise that leads him to his death but wins the audience's esteem.

Any reading of the play that insists on Ajax' integrity has to grapple with his so-called 'deception speech' (646–92) in which he appears to abandon his determination to commit suicide, speaking with unforgettable pathos of the changing nature of the world in which we live as he says that he will submit to the sons of Atreus:

> They are rulers, and so we must give in. Of course. The dread and mightiest powers yield to the appointed authorities. In this way winters thick with snow give place to fruitful summer; and the dark circle of the night makes room for the day with her white horses to kindle light; and the breath of terrible winds lulls the moaning sea to slumber; and, like the rest, all-mastering sleep first binds, then looses, and does not keep his hold for ever. And we – how can we fail to learn good sense? (668–77)

He appears to have given up his thoughts of suicide but the reality is otherwise.

I am reminded of the scene in Shakespeare's *Antony and Cleopatra* when Antony, devastated by his defeats and soon about to fall Ajax-like upon his sword, thinks of the shifting shapes of the clouds:

> Sometime we see a cloud that's dragonish,
> A vapour sometime like a bear or lion,
> A tower'd citadel, a pendent rock,
> A forkèd mountain, or blue promontory
> With trees upon't that nod unto the world
> And mock our eyes with air. (4.15.2–7)

He feels that the 'dislimning' of the clouds reflects his own indistinctness:

> Here I am Antony,
> Yet cannot hold this visible shape ... (4.14.13–14)

In his deception speech, Ajax *explores* the ideas of shifts, of changes, of cycles, of the world's mutability, but it can never be more than an exploration. For unlike Antony, he has rediscovered his rock-like stability of character. Even as he entertains, indeed plays with the ideas of change, the audience, with its knowledge of the myth, – unlike the chorus, whose subsequent outburst of joy tears at the heart-strings – knows that he himself is incapable of it. It is simply impossible to believe that this archetype of manliness has been feminized, as he claims has happened at 651 ('I have been made a woman in my speech'). After all, his iron-like firmness of character is what we admire in him. Take him for all in all, he is a man.

In a play that so pervasively explores the nature of manhood, what are we to make of Ajax' half-brother Teucer? Do his illegitimacy, his mixed ethnicity (he has a Greek father and a Trojan mother) and his allegedly servile status (1235, 1260 and 1289) plus the fact that he is a bowman, fighting from a distance, and not a hoplite (a heavy-armed soldier – 1120–2), justify for the audience the taunt of unmanliness (*kakandriā*) that he envisages his father levelling against him (1013–15)? Absolutely not. Ajax has the confidence in him to entrust him with the future of his son (562–3, 568–70), whom, incidentally, the father wishes to be a clone of himself (550–1). He presides touchingly over the family group surrounding Ajax' corpse during the play's last movement and he sustains his determination to bury his brother in the face of the two big Greek guns, Agamemnon and Menelaus, with an unremitting determination and an emotional and mental energy that are truly magnificent. Then his generous acknowledgement of Odysseus' rôle in ensuring that burial is both impressive and moving. We shall return to it later.

With regard to Tecmessa, the play's one mortal woman, it is hard not to see her as the victim of the male values that the play so constantly asserts. Ajax loves her, as we are assured by the supportive chorus of his sailors (211–12); he praises her for keeping their son safe from him in his madness (536); and there is no reason to disbelieve him when he says that he pities her for her plight if she were to be widowed of him (652–3). He does, however, expect complete submission from her. When he was about to embark on his slaughter of the cattle, she tells us that she asked him where he was going.

> But he answered me in the brief but oft-sung refrain: 'Woman, silence is an adornment for women.' And I learnt my lesson and said no more. (292–4)

The repetition of the word for woman (*gunē*) here and his sharp rebukes at 579–80 and 585–95 (584 for 'sharp') emphasize the fact that a repressive male is laying down the ground rules for female behaviour.

Later Sophocles bases Tecmessa's heart-stopping speech in which she pleads with Ajax to stay alive for the sake of herself and their son, on the celebrated exchange between Andromache and her husband Hector in *Iliad* 6 (407–65). There Andromache expresses her total dependence on Hector and begs him not to go out onto the battlefield. After replying that his sense of shame demands that he must fight, Hector visualizes her fate after the sack of Troy, imagining a Greek taunting her as the wife of Hector when she has been reduced to slavery. In his rehandling of this passage, Sophocles replicates much of the original but there is a key difference. What in Homer is a dialogue between a man and a woman who love each other deeply is reproduced by Sophocles as a single speech delivered by Tecmessa. Ajax is denied the role of the loving Hector. And when Tecmessa has finished, the following dialogue ensues.

> CHORUS. Ajax, I wish that pity touched your heart as it does mine. If it did, you would praise this woman's words.
> AJAX. So far as I am concerned, she shall certainly have my approval if she simply behaves well and brings herself to do what I tell her.

TECMESSA. Yes, of course, dear Ajax, I shall obey in all things.

AJAX. Then bring my son to me so that I may see him. (525–30)

After the warm emotion that permeates Tecmessa's great speech, this exchange strikes a chill to the heart. The point is rammed home that, unlike Homer's Troy, the Greek camp of Sophocles' play is uncompromisingly a man's world.

Three characters await discussion. Two of them need not detain us for very long. Menelaus, so sympathetic an individual in the *Iliad*, comes across as a blustering bully, contemptible in his contemptuousness and fully deserving of the description, 'a nothing' (1114). Agamemnon is less despicable, partly because he is clearly more dangerous; but his extraordinarily offensive abuse of the brothers Teucer and Ajax (1226–63) is decidedly alienating, above all when it descends to the naked racism of his request to have an interpreter present in view of the incomprehensibility of the half-Trojan Teucer's – as he claims – barbarous Greek. Nobility and generosity of spirit are entirely absent from his make-up. He expresses his instinctive unwillingness to fuse kingship with religion, justice and honour when he asserts that 'it is not easy for a king to be pious' (1350). This is surely one of the most disgraceful utterances by a monarch in Greek tragedy. Even if he is partly redeemed by his eventual compliance, gracelessly though it is given (1370–3), when Odysseus urges him to allow Ajax a funeral, he, like his brother, is a hollow man, grossly overparted in his rôle as commander-in-chief.

Before we move on from the sons of Atreus, we should perhaps pause briefly upon a bizarre exchange between Menelaus and Teucer at 1126–7. To the former's question, 'Is it just that this man [Ajax] should prosper after killing me?', the latter replies, 'Killing you? That's a strange thing you've said, if you are actually alive when you have died.' An ancient commentator was right when he remarked that such an exchange was 'more at home in comedy than tragedy' (scholion on 1127). In the language of the latter medium Menelaus, a murder target, is perfectly entitled to refer to himself as 'dead': compare the close parallels at 1291, 1300 and 1500 of Euripides, *Ion*. Thus Teucer's literal-minded assertion that he has said something strange does indeed smack of the world of comedy. Indeed throughout the vigorous cut and thrust of the exchanges in which Teucer and Odysseus see off Menelaus and Agamemnon, we meet with resonances of the scenes in Aristophanic comedy in which intruders interrupt a new state of affairs. For example, in the comic playwright's *Birds* the hero's attempts to complete the sacrifice for his new city are delayed by a succession of individuals on the make, all of whom are sent packing (903–1057 – there are similar sequences later in the play as well as in *Acharnians, Clouds, Peace* and *Wasps*.) If an aura of comic dismissal pervades these scenes in *Ajax*, it may be that it not only adds to the contempt we feel for the sons of Atreus but it also prepares, with something of the lowering of dramatic intensity of the comic episodes in Shakespeare's tragedies, for the deeply serious and emotionally heightened exchange that will follow them.

Finally we turn to Odysseus, who is, of course, the most famous 'man' (*anēr*) of Greek literature. The first word of the *Odyssey* is *andra*, the word for 'man' in the accusative ('Tell me, Muse, of the *man*', i.e. Odysseus), a form in which it occurs 25 times in our play; and the chorus bitterly assert his Odyssean identity when they refer to him as a 'much-enduring man', employing one of his Homeric epithets, in line 956. Does this quintessential Greek man represent an ideal of manhood in Sophocles' tragedy?

It seems to me that he very emphatically does. It is not simply that he never puts a foot wrong. His goodness is far more positive than that. It proves infectious and allows the play to win through to a satisfying closure. At the outset he has perforce to accept that, from the day he was awarded the arms of Achilles, Ajax has been his enemy (18, 78, 104 and 122) but he tries hard to distance himself from the sadistic glee with which the goddess Athena gloats over the pathetic pass to which she has reduced him. In a fine passage, he movingly expresses a sense of a shared humanity with the ruined hero:

> I pity him in his misery despite the fact that he is my enemy, because he has been yoked fast to a dreadful doom. I am thinking of my own lot as much as his. For I see that we are nothing but phantoms, all of us who are alive, or an empty shadow. (121–6)

When he reappears at the end of the play, he finds that for him the distinction between friend and enemy, so consistently harped upon, has been blurred. He pays a handsome tribute to Ajax (1339–41) and authoritatively asserts pious values when he says that it is a violation of the laws of the gods to pursue one's hatred for a good man beyond his death (1343–5). As we have remarked, he persuades Agamemnon to allow the burial of Ajax to proceed.

Now, in a passage shot through with wonderful delicacy of feeling and magnanimity on both sides, Odysseus offers Teucer his friendship and expresses his willingness to participate in the funeral rites. Deeply moved, Teucer responds to his generosity of spirit:

> Noble Odysseus, I have only praise to give you for your words; and you have greatly belied my expectations. You were the worst enemy among the Argives to this man [Ajax], yet you alone stood by him with active help; you could not harden yourself, when he was dead and you alive, to see such great injury done to him. (1381–5)

The two former enemies reach out to each other with sincere emotion.

However, Teucer is aware that the spirit of Ajax would not welcome the participation of Odysseus in his final rites. His brother had died with his hatred unappeased and we know him well enough to be sure that he would have been incapable of bridging the abyss of enmity as Teucer and Odysseus have. So Teucer gently declines Odysseus' offer – the latter takes no offence – and then in a final response to his new friend's nobility he invites him to attend the funeral and to bring someone with him if he wishes. His last line to Odysseus runs: 'Know that in our judgement you are a good man.' The word for 'man' (*anēr*, of course) is placed emphatically at the start of the line (1399).

It is a deeply affecting scene. The human decency and – dare I say it in an ancient context? – chivalry of both of the characters are most sensitively and powerfully conveyed. Teucer responds magnificently to Odysseus' generosity of spirit. Yet if one is to award a palm for great-heartedness to one of them, it must surely be to Odysseus for it was he who launched the process of reconciliation, thus enabling the rites that conclude the play. The nobility that suffuses the exchange between Odysseus and Teucer calls to mind the conclusion of Chaucer's *Franklin's Tale* in which a husband's magnanimity acts like a magnet, leading his wife's would-be lover and then a philosopher to corresponding displays of 'gentil' behaviour. ('Thus kan a squier doon a gentil dede / As well as kan a knight ...' – *Canterbury Tales*, V(F) 1543–4). Teucer is profoundly right to call Odysseus 'a good man', and in this particular play there can be no higher praise.

Indeterminate theatrical space?

There are only five occasions in extant Greek tragedy when the chorus exit from the *orchēstra* and leave the audience looking at an empty stage. One of them marks the clear-cut change of scene in

Aeschylus' *Eumenides* when the action moves from Delphi to Athens (at 234). Another, in the probably non-Euripidean *Rhesus* (at 564), precedes a dialogue scene involving four actors. Two more instances come at Euripides' *Alcestis* 746[6] and his *Helen* 385. At both of these moments, the vacancy is the prelude to the respective entries of a comic character and a bizarre-looking one, in the first case a servant describing the antics of the drunken Heracles, in the second Menelaus in his grotesque costume made up of flotsam and jetsam from his ship. The fifth of these entries onto an empty and silent stage is that of Ajax after line 814 of Sophocles' play.

It is at this line that Tecmessa, the Messenger and the two sections of the chorus leave the stage. Silence follows. Ajax enters and delivers his 'suicide speech'. If we omit tragic prologues from the reckoning – they have their own agenda in their direct communication with the audience – the three speeches that follow the above-mentioned moments after the stage has emptied are three of Greek tragedies' four soliloquies. (The fourth is the great speech of Prometheus in the possibly Aeschylean play of that name which comes after the opening scene but before the entry of the chorus (88–126).) And there is certainly nothing comic or bizarre about the soliloquy that Ajax delivers. It has a truly Shakespearean range and intensity.

An aspect of the staging of *Ajax* that has been the subject of much recent discussion concerns the location in which Ajax speaks his 'suicide speech'. After the exit of the chorus and Tecmessa, does the scene change 'to some deserted place', as Ajax indicates that it will at 657 (an 'untrodden place') and an ancient commentator asserts in his note on 815? Does it become more specifically 'a lonely spot on the sea-shore, with trees or bushes', as Richard Jebb supposes, referring to the 'grove' of 892 (cf. 654–7)? Or does it not change at all but remain outside Ajax' tent, as Scott Scullion argues in his interesting and informative book on the dramaturgy of Greek tragedy (Scullion, 1994)?

The confusion is understandable – the text is hard to pin down – but I do not feel that this betokens dramatic incompetence on Sophocles' part. For me the question to be asked is whether we should be searching for a specific location at all. We are after all dealing with the unlocalized stage of Greek tragedy. Scenery was probably minimal and the geography of the plays was largely conjured up by the words that the actors speak. Richard Green and Eric Handley (1995) draw attention, for example, to the verbal scene-painting at the start of Sophocles' *Oedipus at Colonus* which creates in the mind's eye of the audience distant city walls, a nearby grove with laurel, olive and vines, where nightingales sing, 'a sacred place, it seems' (14–18). It is by such means that a Greek play's location is generally identified; but surely there is no logical reason why it cannot be indeterminate and the dramatic space can become a theatrical no man's land. In our play Ajax enters onto an empty stage and calls upon Zeus, Hermes, the Furies, the Sun and Death. Why should an audience be concerned about, even think about where he is standing when he invokes these divine and elemental forces? Ajax then calls upon his native Salamis, upon Athens and the springs, rivers and plains of Troy. In his imagination – and in that of the audience – he can visit those places: they can become the successive locations of his last moments on earth. Significantly his final invocations are addressed to a far wider geography of Troy than the area in front of his tent. The location of the soliloquy is wherever the audience feel that Ajax' words suggest it is.

Scullion believes that the setting of Greek tragedy, quite differently from the flexible, fluid theatrical space of comedy, is straightfor-wardly naturalistic: it 'will retain the identity established for it'. However, if Ajax is liberated from a confining location, he can travel on an imaginative journey that is, in dramatic terms, a real one at the same time. It may be that the alchemy of drama and Sophocles' fine use of the unlocalized stage are working together here to wonderfully expressive effect.

If this is the right way of looking at this matter, the play will remain unlocalized for the rest of its duration. There is certainly evidence that they are some way from the tent when Teucer asks Tecmessa to fetch her son Eurysaces from there (985–8) and she reappears with the boy after almost 200 lines. It is because of the absence of any specific setting, that Ajax' corpse, inescapably present on stage from at least 915, and nothing else will prove to be the focal point of the action. In a sense it will become the play's set, the subject of the quarrels that will rage over the dead hero and the visual emblem of his greatness.

CHAPTER 3

WOMEN OF TRACHIS

THE HEART OF DARKNESS

A frequently noted feature of *Women of Trachis* is that the same actor would have played not only the fragile Deianeira but Heracles, her now brutish husband, as well. These are two of the most remarkable roles in Sophocles. To perform both of them represents a challenge of a totally different order from that, say, facing the third actor (the tritagonist) who acted the old Messenger, the old Nurse and the Old Man, clearly a specialist in antique characters as Shakespeare is supposed to have been. Sophocles was surely writing for a virtuoso actor who he felt could convey the hesitant femininity of the one and the harsh masculinity of the other with equal conviction.

As with the actor, so with the play. An important part of its aim, we may well feel, is to set up contrasts between the female and the male. The female presence is certainly very strong. The action opens, uniquely in Sophocles' surviving plays, with a long soliloquy by a woman. The chorus consists of women as in only one other of the extant plays (*Electra*), here the maidens of Trachis; and Deianeira clearly bonds with them. This is especially evident in the passage where she consults them about the wisdom of sending the anointed tunic to Heracles and they encourage her to go ahead (586–93). A procession of captive women appears at 225, causing one of the greatest accumulations of women on the stage in surviving Greek tragedy. Though the captive princess Iole, the latest object of

Heracles' lust, says not a word, there is a wonderful concentration on her. The spotlight shows her weeping in her misery (326) but her feelings are otherwise almost completely opaque – and this may well cause an audience to speculate all the more on what her emotions towards Heracles may be. Apart from her evident nobility (309) and her presumed sensibility (463–7), all we know about her is that her beauty has destroyed her life and her country (466–7). Deianeira too is the victim of her own beauty (25–30), another trophy of conquest. At the end of the tragedy – a small point – it seems likely that the women go off to the mountain rather than tamely entering the palace (1275). They thus draw attention to themselves by countering the audience's expectation. Before the start, Heracles has been the slave of the Lydian queen Omphale. And, of course, the whole devastating action unravelled in the play is the consequence of the loveliness of two women, Deianeira and Iole.

The emphasis on the feminine is evident above all in the characterization of the former. This is perhaps the most delicate and detailed portrayal of any woman in Greek tragedy, with the possible exception of Creusa in Euripides' *Ion*. What makes its depth the more remarkable is that she leaves the play two thirds of the way through, yet Sophocles needs no more space to develop his complex creation. We know her well. Her opening soliloquy is on one level exposition, telling us how she became Heracles' wife. It also makes very clear to us the terrible insecurities to which she is prey:

> When I still lived in the house of my father Oeneus in Pleuron I had a more grievous dread of marriage than any other Aetolian girl. My suitor was a river god, I'm speaking of Achelous, who asked my father for me in three shapes. He came in visible form, sometimes as a bull, sometimes as a shimmering, writhing snake, sometimes as a human torso with a bull's head with cascades of river water flowing from his dark beard. With

such a husband to look forward to, I was forever praying in
my misery that I would die before I ever got near to his bed.
But later, to my joy, there came the famous son of Zeus and
Alcmena who fell to battle with him and freed me ... Zeus, the
decider of the contest, brought a happy issue, if indeed it was
happy. For ever since I married Heracles as his chosen bride, I
have been nursing one fear after another as I worry about him.
(6–21 and 26–9)

It is scarcely surprising that, faced with the prospect of marriage
with the river god, she longs for death. Achelous is a terrifying
suitor. But he is more than that. Manifesting himself to her as
a bull, a snake and a watery minotaur, he is pretty obviously a
symbol of rampant male sexuality. She cannot bear to watch the
fight between Heracles and Achelous (21–5). The chorus revisit this
appalling conflict at 503–30, laying further emphasis on its sexual
nature. Eulektros Kypris (Aphrodite who brings wedded happiness)
acts as umpire, while Deianeira sits on a distant hill helplessly
awaiting the victor of the encounter. Whichever of the two wins, he
will be violently and aggressively male. She is terrified of everything
and these fears largely focus on her sexuality. Yet while she leads
us to believe that before marriage she was terrified of sex, her
relationship with Heracles has clearly been sexually fulfilling. She
has had four children by him and she still loves him and wants to be
loved by him (631–2). Before her suicide, she goes into the bedroom
she had shared with him and puts blankets on her marriage bed and
then bids a very tearful farewell to it (912–22), just like Alcestis,
the 'good wife' in Euripides (*Alcestis*, 175–88). However, despite her
sexual fulfilment, there is a heart-rending nostalgia as she tells the
virginal chorus of her own virgin youth:

Young life is nurtured in places of its own and neither the heat
of the sun god nor the rain nor any of the winds disturbs it. On

the contrary, it grows untroubled amid pleasures until the time
when a woman is called a wife instead of a virgin and takes her
portion of anxieties in the night time, fearing for her husband
or children. (144–50)

Her beauty has been a burden to her, causing the centaur Nessus
to attempt to rape her (564–5). This alarming event took place in a
truly liminal place, the middle of the river Euenos which Deianeira
was crossing on her way with Heracles from her father's house to
his – and to the consummation of their marriage (562–3). She
suffered sexual abuse on the very day on which she was to lose her
maidenhood. Unsurprisingly she speculates on whether Heracles
has had sex with Iole or not, coming to the conclusion that he
has (536) – rightly so as Heracles reveals at 1225–6. A Freudian
psychiatrist would have a field day here.

She shows a wonderful sensitivity towards, and empathy with,
the captives, especially Iole, who proves to be most sensationally a
victim of rape. (Heracles has sacked her city, killed all its men and
enslaved all its women in order to possess her (282–4).) Yet Iole's
presence in her house becomes a source of terrible sexual insecurity
for Deianeira as she faces the fact that her rival's beauty has still
to reach its prime while hers is on the wane (547–8). Speaking
bitterly of the two of them awaiting Heracles' embrace under one
blanket, she asks who could endure to share her husband with the
younger woman (539–40 and 545–6). Her restless insecure mind
cannot find a lasting foothold. Does anyone in Greek tragedy ask
more questions than she? She is liable to qualify any statement that
she makes. A striking example of this comes when she believes (in
fact mistakenly) that all is well and Heracles is returning home in
triumph:

CHORUS: Lady, now you have clear cause for joy both in the
    present circumstances and in what you have been told.

DEIANEIRA: How could I fail to be happy – and most rightly so
too – when I hear of this success of my husband? Of course
happiness must run with success. Nevertheless, it is natural
for those who judge well to fear for the man who fares well
in case he later takes a fall. For a terrible pity swept over me,
my friends, when I saw these ill-fated women ... (291–9)

After tentatively grasping at joy, she has slipped into sad reflections
on the instability of fortune and then into sympathy for her
husband's victims. She goes on to express her fears for her own
children (303–6), a crucial aspect of her personality. Deianeira has
a vast capacity for love, but life has left her racked by anxiety and
insomnia (29–30, 149 and 175–6).

This startlingly modern characterization is all the more remarkable
when one considers the other two female Sophoclean protagonists,
Antigone and Electra. Possessed of a massive self-confidence and
sureness, they are largely unable to relate to anyone else except
on their own terms. Self-doubt is not in their repertoire. To think
of that formidable pair makes it clear how original a creation the
fragile, deeply feminine Deianeira was for this particular dramatist.
Their personalities offer them a compass which shows them their
way; hers singularly fails to.

So in a very fundamental sense the play establishes a feminine
world to set against the masculine principle represented above all
by Heracles. Heracles has civilized the world – he looks back on his
labours in an outburst of tremendous power (1089–1102) – but,
amid his agonizing spasms of pain, the civilizer appears a brute.
He is appalled by the fact that it is a woman who has caused his
destruction (1062–3). He never acknowledges that he has misjudged
his wife. He is a serial rapist (459–60) and an absentee father (31–5)
whose essential nature as we see it in this play marks him out as an
adversary of the feminine principle.

This alarming iconic presentation throws into relief the sensitive portrayal of his son, the temperately masculine Hyllus. He appears at the beginning, middle and end of the play and there is a sense in which he holds it together. The child of a desperately insecure mother and a distant but idolized brute of a father, he is a young man undergoing a rite of passage through a terrifying process. The final scene, in which Heracles pressures him into agreeing first to play a key role in killing him (1193–1215) and then to marry Iole, the cause (however innocently) of his parents' doom (1219–51), is charged with almost unbearable intensity and horror. Even so, this is the end of the route by which Hyllus comes to manhood.

The play has many themes. It is full of ideas of travel which look forward to the final journey to the top of Mount Oeta. The wide world of Heracles' travels is now limited to the very specific geography of this small area of north Greece, just as the slow passage of the fifteen months that have preceded the action of the play comes to a hideous climax in just one terrible day. The sickness of love is stressed again and again and becomes inseparable from the physical corrosion visited on Heracles by Nessus' ointment. Love in classical literature is rarely life-enhancing for long – that between Odysseus and Penelope in the *Odyssey* is the exception that proves the rule – but it is seldom shown in as grim a light as in this tragedy.

A theme of particular interest in *Women of Trachis* is that of communication – or rather the lack of it. At the outset Deianeira is anxious about where Heracles may be. Her son Hyllus, who has been living in the same palace, knows the answer and hasn't yet told her. For her part, she has not told him about an oracle concerning Heracles till now. Heracles himself only realizes the true meaning of the oracle near the end of the play and of his life (1164–73). The words of the dying centaur Nessus are riddling and misleading and Deianeira is crazy to accept them at face value. Then

Hyllus and Heracles both hopelessly misjudge her. The channels of communication are constantly blocked or corrupted.

This failure to communicate is most clearly apparent in the extraordinary scene in which the Messenger and Lichas talk to Deianeira. First of all the Messenger comes on (180), eager for a tip to reward his happy news (191). But the strange thing is that he does not deliver the messenger speech. The audience's legitimate expectation is frustrated. It is left to Lichas to plug the gap with his grossly misleading account of events (prompted by his wish to spare his mistress's feelings (480–2)). The Messenger knows that he is being decidedly economical with the reality and he presumably indicates something of this by gesture and movement while Lichas is talking. When Lichas has left the stage, the Messenger tells Deianeira the truth. We in the audience have misjudged him. He is not after all an opportunistic seeker of tips but an honest man (373–4). Now the Messenger and Deianeira force a wriggling Lichas to come out with the reality. However, she then deludes herself into believing that she can come to terms with the fact that her husband is being unfaithful. And then again, the silent Iole could have told a dreadful story but communicates nothing but sorrow.

Thus the characters – the audience too – have to pick their way through a quicksand of misunderstanding. Does the play have an essential reality, a fundamental truth to offer? I suggest that it does. As his journey nears its end, we are confronted with the icon of terrible pain and torment that is Heracles. There is a parallel here with King Lear on the heath amid the storm in Shakespeare's play. Seeing the naked figure of Edgar who is pretending to be a lunatic, Lear meditates:

Is man no more than this? Consider him well. Thou owest the worm no silk, the beast no hide, the sheep no wool, the cat no perfume.- Ha, here's three on 's are sophisticated; thou art the thing itself. (3.4.96–100)

Wishing to reduce himself to what one might call the naked truth, Lear then tries to take off his clothes, only to be stopped by the Fool.

In a similar way, Heracles flings off his covering:

Off with the coverings! Look, all of you, at the spectacle of my wretched body, see the unhappy man and his pitiable state. (1078–80).

He is not totally naked but the poisoned tunic sticks to his skin showing every joint (767–9). This is the effect the poison had on the tuft of wool:

It completely disintegrated and crumbled into a powder on the ground. To look at it was most like the sawdust you would see when wood is cut. That's what the tuft I had thrown away was like. But out of the earth on which it lay exposed, clots of foam bubbled up like the rich juice of the blue-ripe grapes from Bacchus' vine when it is poured on the earth. (698–704)

As Heracles writhes in the hideous pain of the poison that ravens on his body and drinks his blood, he invites the audience to view him as a spectacle (1079 – the Greek word *theásthe* (view) is from the same root as *theátron* (theatre)). Now at last there is no failure of communication. What his father Zeus has allowed to happen to his son is only too horribly clear. The play's last line, 'And there is nothing of these things that is not Zeus', rings out with a terrible resonance. Heracles' agonized torso is 'the thing itself'.

So eventually the horrific reality has been confronted. Can Heracles now rebuild himself in any way? He does in fact win through to a kind of calm as he faces and accepts the truth of his situation. To be burnt on Mount Oeta offers a kind of completion, an end to his pain, his labours and his travels – and to the fulfilment of oracles. Terrible things still lie ahead, as we have seen, with the demands Heracles makes of his son; but there is at least a sense of closure.

However, a key problem remains. The myth of Heracles, a son of Zeus (19 and 826), generally ends with his deification. Consumed in the fire on Oeta, he becomes a god. Yet there is no mention of this in Sophocles' play. Some critics believe that it is so fundamental a part of the myth that the audience will simply assume that it will happen. Since it is impossible to prove or disprove this belief, it would be comforting to go along with P.E. Easterling, one of the best commentators on the play, who writes, 'Fortunately this is not the most important question.' But it surely *is*. If deification does follow the cremation on Mount Oeta, the terrible suffering undergone by Heracles in the play has a degree of compensation.

My own view is that it does not. Greek dramatists generally take pains to activate the aspects of a myth that they want their audience to respond to. Very conspicuously Sophocles says nothing at all to suggest that deification is in any way a possibility. It may or may not be relevant that Euripides in his Heracles play causes the hero to forswear the world of the gods and the paternity of Zeus and to find salvation in human friendship. Easterling quotes *Iliad* 18.117–19: 'No, not even mighty Heracles escaped death, who was dearest to Lord Zeus, son of Cronos, but fate and the dire wrath of Hera subdued him.' The bleakness of that statement – Heracles died and his father, the king of the gods, could not save him: no hint of deification here – is given further emphasis in Sophocles' play, in which, near the start (139–40), the chorus exhort Deianeira to be hopeful 'since who has seen Zeus so unmindful for his children?' They are profoundly mistaken. There *is* closure to be sure, but for me the play remains unutterably bleak and terrifying.

CHAPTER 4

ANTIGONE

THE MARTYR AND THE KING

S ome good critics have viewed the Creon of this tragedy as an intemperate tyrant, while others have branded Antigone a fanatic, inflammatory in speech and disruptive in behaviour. A due regard for dramatic economy, however, may suggest that Sophocles would have been unlikely to present either protagonist as solely responsible for the play's catastrophe. Certainly many have been attracted by the nineteenth-century German philosopher G.W.F. Hegel's belief (here summarized by Mark Griffith) that 'both Creon and Antigone are right in principle, but that each of their conflicting principles is of only limited validity, whereas each of them insists on its absolute claims'. Hegel is of course correct when he goes on to say that the tragic conflict destroys them both; but we may have our doubts as to whether the play can support his conclusion that it 'results in the emergence of an ethically "higher" and more inclusive plane of consciousness'. Be that as it may, to see the play as a conflict between two eminently justifiable but ultimately limited ideals, makes very good dramatic sense; but that does not necessary mean that it is a justified reading.

Is it possible to reach an objective conclusion on the matter? Surely, whatever her critics may say, Antigone simply *is* right. The gods (we must infer), men and even Creon in the end pronounce her so. Yet there is much about her that makes her appear harsh and inflexible. Creon has taken power after a battle that could have brought destruction to the city. Surely he is right to insist on the observance of his first decree. His treatment of Polyneices' corpse would not, it appears, have struck Athenians as unduly severe. Nobody, not even Antigone, disputes that he was a traitor; and Athenian law decreed that traitors should be refused burial within Attica. (While their families could bury them abroad, this does not usually seem to have happened.)[7] Decidedly more contentious is his execution of Antigone by live burial and starvation. This was certainly not a regular punishment but it seems likely that his hope that the supply of some food and water would avert responsibility and pollution, though tragically mistaken (1068–9), would not have been thought absurd. He surely resists interpretation as a deep-dyed villain.

How do the play's internal audiences, the chorus and the minor characters, view the protagonists? We may find in their reactions a compass with which to guide our own. The chorus of elders – and indeed their age is stressed (159, 281 and 1092–3) – are fundamentally Creon's men. Their jubilant greeting of the sun that heralds the day after the failed onslaught of arrogant and impious forces upon their city creates an ineffaceable impression of a rebirth for Thebes under its new king (100–54 and 155–7). Later they refrain from expressing approval of Creon's initial decree (211–14) and they suggest that the attempt at burial may be 'god-driven' (278–9), but they certainly do not communicate the well-spring of popular support for Antigone that both the heroine herself (509) and Haemon (692–700) are confident exists. Although they later take control of the situation, giving Creon guidance (1091–1107) and eventually blaming him (1260), they come across as essentially loyal, by no means cowed subjects. And while they feel great pity for Antigone (especially at 801–5), they never express approval of what she has done. On the contrary, they see her as a savage daughter of a savage father (471–2). The justly famous choral ode in which they celebrate the wondrous achievements of man and his potential use of his talents for the good or bad of the city, finds very little space for the religious dimension of human life to which, as the audience well knows, Antigone is now utterly committed (332–75; there are only three words about the gods apart from Hades (369)).

If we are justified in seeing the chorus as essentially Creon's men, what about the minor characters? Ismene, whose rational timidity makes her a foil for Antigone's uncompromising heroism, feels that her sister should recognize her weakness as a woman and bow to the inevitable (61–7). Though she later hopes to die with Antigone, it may well be a mistake to read this expression of sororal solidarity and love as a belated acknowledgement that her sister has behaved rightly all along (540–1 and 548). When the Guard makes his appearances, it is as if Bottom is breaking in irrepressibly from *A Midsummer Night's Dream*. This comic Everyman's warm sympathy for Antigone – he feels she has become a friend (438–9) – is a striking touch, but it means little when balanced against his instinct for survival (439–40) and nowhere does this man of the people say she was right.

In the brilliant scene between Haemon and Creon, the hot-blooded son shows amazing self-control as he tries a number of different approaches to make it clear to his father that Antigone is in the right while he is wrong and should therefore yield. Now that we are half-way through the play, a minor character is for the first time speaking up loud and clear in opposition to Creon and in support of Antigone. Moreover, in Teiresias' terrifying interview with Creon, this point of view is given divine endorsement. The hideous pollution resulting from Creon's actions has infected many more Greek cities than Thebes itself (1080–3). Then, after the communicative silence of her exit, we are told that Eurydice holds Creon responsible for Haemon's death (1305 and 1312–13). The weight of the play's judgement has swung firmly against him. He is seen as tragically guilty of *hamartiā* (1024–5, 1260 and 1261 – Aristotle, *Poetics* 1453a: see glossary). Antigone's heroism now shines bright.

Surely this shift in the way Creon is viewed in the tragedy is reflected in Sophocles' development of his character. Having started the play as a king doing his level best to re-establish order in a state which had come frighteningly close to destruction, he is subjected to pressures and challenges that undermine his personality until, as Haemon says, he is only fit to be king of an unpopulated land (739).

It may be that the seeds of his decline already lie in his opening proclamation. As we have seen (p. 37), Athenian law refused burial to traitors. However, was it necessary also to forbid lamentation for Polyneices and to state specifically that birds and dogs would eat his corpse (204–6; cf. 27–30)? This grisly addendum may smack of hubristic gloating. As yet, however, the jury must be out on Creon's behaviour. But he soon appears to invite judgement on his performance as ruler:

> It is impossible to know a man completely, his character, his mentality and his judgement, until he has been seen to be tested in holding office and making laws. (175–7)

Audiences will not be slow to take him up on this challenge. Creon's instinctively negative reaction when the chorus suggest that the attempted burial may be heaven-driven (278–9) is a prelude to much that is to come. It also gives us a hint of the anger latent in him (280), which will subsequently prove so disastrous. In his great scene with Antigone, he sounds ever more tyrannical and his repeated passionate insistence that a man must not be worsted by a woman (525, 648–9 and 678–80) may suggest an underlying insecurity, as may his fear of his enemies' laughter (647). Next there follows what must strike every audience as his crazy assumption and continuing belief that Ismene is an active participant in civil disobedience (488–90 and 531–5). (It is surely a sign of grace, on the other hand, that he extracts himself from this folly at 771.) Then the line in which he brushes aside his son's engagement to Antigone, saying that there are other fields for him to plough (569), takes the breath away with its offensive crudity. And his instruction that she should be dragged out so that she can be killed in Haemon's presence shows him as a cliché tyrant out-heroding Herod (760–1). According to Antigone (35–6), he had originally decreed that any violation of his edict should be punished by public stoning. When he changes the punishment to a living entombment (773–6), this may be in recognition of the fact that the city would not give him the support that the communal infliction of stoning demands. Then he is guilty of shocking blasphemy when he declares to Teiresias that he will not bury Polyneices:

> You will not hide that man in a grave, not even if Zeus' eagles are willing to snatch him up and carry him as food to Zeus' throne. (1039–41)

Of course he acknowledges his error and tries desperately to put things right. Yet even now he shows a tragic misunderstanding of the priorities: disastrously he goes against the chorus' advice (1100–1) and sees to the burial of the corpse before attempting to free Antigone. It remains true that he has learnt a lesson (1272); but sundered from his family in the vast shipwreck of all he held dear, he feels that everything is 'askew' (1345). He wishes to be led out of the way (1321, 1339). He has been reduced to nothing (1325).

Yet if Creon's story is a grim saga of decline, that should not lead us to believe that Antigone is an embodiment of perfection. A martyr she may be but she is scarcely a saint. Her cruelty to her sister, who lacks her single-minded clarity of vision, can prove painful to an audience, though it is possible for the actor playing her to deliver 559–60 in a loving and sympathetic way:

> Courage! You are alive, but my life was over long ago: I want to serve the dead.

Even so, while her signature line which has resonated down the ages, 'I was not born to join in hate but in love' (523), may move us deeply, at the same time it stirs in us the uncomfortable awareness that the only person she is willing to join with in love is her dead brother. In a notorious and for some an alienating passage probably borrowed from Herodotus (3.119), she admits that she would not have done what she did for a child or a husband (905–12).[8] For all that, for all her harshness, her inflexibility, her narrowness of focus, her cause is a great one and her speech which champions the gods' unwritten laws against political diktats (450–70) is as soul-stirring as anything in dramatic literature. Not only in our hearts but in our guts, we know that she is right. When I saw *Antigone* in the theatre of Herodes Atticus on the first night of the Athens Festival in 1970, Greece was ruled by a military junta. In response to the heroine's passionate speech, the audience went wild, launching salvo upon salvo of applause. The message was not lost on the brass hats in the front row. Soon afterwards the play was banned.

Aristotle pronounced that a tragedy is an imitation of an action (*Poetics* 1450a) and it does indeed seem that his dictum applies to most of the works in the genre that have come down to us. But are there *two* actions in this play? The destinies of Antigone and Creon are, of course, inextricably linked, and in the section which concludes this chapter I suggest that the play succeeds in maintaining its unity while accommodating the tragedies of both protagonists. However, Creon's personal tragedy is certainly the main focus of the play after Antigone's death. His son commits suicide (in a hideous parody of the sexual fulfilment of which he, like Antigone, has been deprived

(1236–9)). His wife Eurydice kills herself while denouncing him. He feels himself to be annihilated (1325). Mark Griffith, the most recent (and an excellent) editor of the play, finds a certain optimism here. Schooled by the lessons of the tragedy, Creon will continue to rule in Thebes, upholding, Griffith believes, 'an order that will henceforth elicit (we are to assume) a more restrained and subdued exercise of paternal authority'. This strikes me as an assumption too far. The play may end with the chorus stating that a lesson can be learnt:

> The mighty words of the arrogant pay the price in great blows
> of fate and thus in old age they teach good sense. (1350–3)

However, as the elders try to insist on closure, their clichés are as inadequate as the banality with which the Messenger concludes his shattering account of Creon's disastrous journey: lack of good counsel, he informs us, is the greatest of evils for mankind (1242–3). In any event, the play refuses to focus on a future for Thebes. There is no hint that Creon has the capacity to rebuild himself. He may have learnt from his tragic experiences and from the tragedy of Antigone, but he has profited nothing.

To return to the question raised in my opening paragraph as to whether the tragedy shows the conflict of two justifiable but limited ideals, the answer must surely be no. It is, of course, helpful to consider what can be approved in Creon's stance and what is rebarbative in Antigone; but the greatness of the latter's spirit, her fierce love for her brother and her devotion to what she knows to be her religious duty win her the audience's hearts and minds. Both Creon and Antigone are tragic figures but it is she who is the avatar of heroism and the palm of victory is hers. Creon discovers that he has become nothing (1325). Devoted to death Antigone may be, but her story is thrillingly life-enhancing.

The double time scheme in *Antigone*

As a footnote to the above chapter, I discuss what strikes me as a highly interesting and significant feature of the play and conclude with the thought that *Antigone* has space to accommodate both the tragedy of its eponymous heroine which, as I have suggested, is at the same time her victory, and that of king Creon which is bleak, dark and, I think, devoid of any hint of consolation.

In three articles published in *Blackwood's Magazine* (November 1849, April and May 1850), one John Wilson, under the *nom de guerre* of Christopher North, propounded the view that Shakespeare's *Othello* operates on a double time scheme. The represented time in Cyprus (Acts 2 to 5) is some thirty-three hours, lasting from about 4 pm on Saturday till the early hours of Monday morning. If we take this time scheme at face value, there has been no opportunity for Desdemona and Cassio to commit adultery: Iago's insinuations and Othello's suspicions are manifestly absurd. However, another time scheme is in operation as well. By its clock, the protagonists have been in Cyprus for more than a week. For example, we find Bianca, a local courtesan, complaining that it has been 'Seven days and nights, / Eightscore-eight hours' (3.4.170–1) since she last saw Cassio, who by the first time scheme had arrived in Cyprus only the day before.[9]

Shakespeare's use of 'long time' enables him to make Iago's gulling of Othello the more convincing, while his 'short time' heightens the claustrophobic intensity of the action as it proceeds so swiftly and remorselessly to its conclusion.

My purpose here is to argue that Sophocles operates a similar double time scheme in *Antigone*. It is, of course, true that those Greek tragedies – the vast majority of them – whose represented time is less than a day tend to be crowded with incident; but in *Antigone* it is not simply the case that a great deal happens. Like

Shakespeare in *Othello*, Sophocles appears to be working with two clocks.

At the outset, the 'short time' of *Antigone* is established with great precision. The play opens before dawn at the end of the very night on which the Argive army has fled the land (15–16). On the previous day that army had been crushingly defeated and the brothers Eteocles and Polyneices had killed each other. The chorus salute the rising sun at 100ff. The morning now moves quickly forward, with the guard speaking of the midday sun and its intense heat in 415–17. And 'short time' leads the action to its shattering conclusion without a break.

Yet there is another more leisurely time scheme at work. We may find ourselves wondering under what circumstances Antigone had heard the news of Creon's edict so early in the morning (7–8), though a plausible scenario could be imagined. (One editor suggests that it was promulgated on the battlefield.) More tellingly, when the Guard arrives, he emphasizes the fact that he has taken his time over his journey, stopping and starting and turning round on the way (225–32). We may also gain the impression that he and his fellows have been on duty for some time: the mention of 'the first day-watchman' (253) suggests a well-established rota.

Further evidence of 'long time' arrives when, in his tirade against the Guard, Creon talks as if men in the city have been objecting to his edict for some time (289–92), though he has only recently delivered it and has, indeed, been king for only a few hours (15–16 and 170–4). Later, when the Guard returns after arresting Antigone, he makes it clear that Polyneices' corpse had started to stink (412). Yet by 'short time' he has only been dead for a night and some of the morning.

In this same scene, Creon, king (I say again) for less than a day, talks as if Antigone and Ismene have been plotting to oust him from his throne for some time (531–3: the imperfect tenses suggest continuing actions) and soon Haemon observes that dark talk against Creon and high praise of Antigone are spreading around the city in secret (692–700). Would 'short time' have allowed a sufficient opportunity for this to happen?

After Antigone has gone off to her death, Teiresias describes the defilement of the city's altars by birds and dogs which have brought to them carrion flesh from the corpse (1016–18). Indeed, he goes on to say that birds and beasts have spread a polluting stench to the cities of the Argive alliance (1080–3). It is certainly far later in the day by now, but even so, 'short time' would call for unconvincingly swift action from the birds and beasts of prey.

By now, I feel, the audience has become accustomed – below the level of consciousness, no doubt – to the play's double time scheme and will feel little or no surprise when some words of Teiresias draw attention to it. While Creon is in fact to lose his son later that very day, the prophet foretells that he will not accomplish 'many rapid cycles of the sun' before he does so (1064–7). Teiresias insists on 'long time'; but the 'short time' scheme proceeds without remission.

What is the effect of the double time scheme? One result may be that Creon is denied a possible line of defence. In 'short time', he makes his very first edict, having taken over the throne of Thebes at a time of great national emergency. Surely he cannot let that decree be violated? As I have suggested above, political stability demands that the new ruler enforce it to the full. But the play's 'long time' makes it seem as if he has ruled for a significant period. One particularly striking example comes in 1164, where we are assured that this king for a day – short time – 'governed [the verb is in the imperfect tense, again suggesting a continuing action], while he flourished with his issue of noble children' – long time. Sophocles does not, it appears, wish to claim for him the justification of a novice ruler asserting himself.

A decidedly more significant effect is that the play conveys the impression that its action is unified through the tragic intensity with which 'short time' propels it forward, while 'long time' gives its two protagonists room in which to breathe. In a single span, Sophocles is conveying the tragedies not only of Antigone but of Creon too. His juggling with clocks gives him space enough and time to allow both of these characters due weight. As 'short time' works itself out relentlessly in a day, the dramatist's 'long time' finds room for the final destinies of not one but two tragic figures. Viewed in this light, any debate over which of them the play is 'really about' may seem to stem from an inadequate response to the technical virtuosity with which Sophocles has composed his *Antigone*.

CHAPTER 5

OEDIPUS THE KING
THE CITY AND THE HOUSE

O *edipus the King* is the most celebrated of all Greek tragedies. Together with Euripides' *Iphigenia among the Taurians*, it is the play cited by Aristotle far more than any other in his *Poetics*. Its plot structure, which ties recognition to reversal, its arousal of pity and fear, and his belief that its hero has a tragic flaw (*hamartiā*) – though no two people can agree exactly what this is –, all these features combine to make *Oedipus* a firm favourite with him. Then, at the very outset of the twentieth century, Sigmund Freud in his *Interpretation of Dreams*, attributed the strong emotion aroused in us by the destiny of Oedipus to the impulse, which he claims is common to all men, to desire their mother and to murder their father. In 1973, George Devereux, following in Freud's footsteps, argued that Oedipus' explanations of his self-blinding are unconvincing rationalizations: the act is to be interpreted as a symbol of self-castration. Other scholars such as Jean-Pierre Vernant (see p. 6) have taken an anthropological approach, suggesting that the play is a stage enactment of the treatment of a scapegoat to purge the community of its accumulated contamination, just as each year at Athens two scapegoats, one on behalf of the men, the other of the women, were expelled to attain purification for the city and avert plagues. Then again, in a brilliant fusion of literary, historical and social analysis (see p. 4), Bernard Knox has argued (a) that *Oedipus the King* is 'a dramatic embodiment of the creative vigour and intellectual daring of the fifth-century Athenian spirit', and (b) that 'the catastrophe of the tragic hero ... becomes the catastrophe of fifth-century man: all his furious energy and intellectual daring drive him on to this terrible discovery of his fundamental ignorance – he is not the measure of all things but the thing measured and found wanting.'

Of course, each of these distinguished interpreters sheds light on the play, but there is, I feel, one respect in which their analyses all fall short. They identify in the tragedy a straight-forward symmetry that I quite simply cannot find there. After all, the problem that the play initially offers Oedipus is how to cure the land and population of a Thebes wasted by pollution and plague, so horrifically conveyed in the words of the Priest of Zeus at the outset:

> Thebes is dying, blighted in the land's fruitful crops, blighted in the grazing herds of cattle and the barren birth pangs of women. Yes, and the fiery god of fever darts down and harries the city with a dreadful plague, emptying the house of Cadmus while black Death is enriched with cries and groans. (25–30)

Oedipus tracks down the source of pollution, viz. himself; and Sophocles could have set his personal disaster against his civic triumph in showing the way to his land's salvation. However, he did not choose to do this. The idea of the sick country, hammered home so repeatedly in the first half of the play, simply disappears after line 685.

A second set-back to the discovery of a neat symmetry follows Apollo's decree (and the scapegoat theorists' expectations) that the killer of Laius should be exiled or killed (100–1). The killer is identified; but this does not does not result in his banishment or death. Despite Oedipus' constant insistence that it should (1410–11, 1436, 1451 and 1518), he is told by Creon that he is an offence to the elements (1424–28) and ordered into the house (1429).

In the 2006 revision of his 1982 Cambridge edition of the play, R.D. Dawe draws attention to both of these challenges to symmetry. He is oddly unfazed by the first; but he feels so passionately about the second that he pronounces the play's final 107 lines spurious. I am reminded of Sheridan's Mr Puff in *The Critic* who, on discovering that the actors have yet again taken the pruning knife to his tragedy, exclaims, 'The pruning knife – zounds the axe!' I rather hope that we can find a way of avoiding Dr Dawe's major surgery. After all, it may be that drama works on other principles than orderliness of design.

Aristotle's praise of the synchronization of the tragic ingredients of recognition (*anagnōrisis*) and reversal (*peripeteia* – *Poetics* 1452a) after 923 is surely justified; but the sophistication with which the dramatist handles these concepts is anything but straightforward. Oedipus comes close to recognition of the solution to the play's initial problem – who killed Laius? – at 738, 744–5 and 754. However, the recognition that Aristotle is talking about, the one that coincides with the reversal, is his realization of who he is, which leads to his determination to blind himself (1182–5). Devastatingly prefaced by the two lines in which the Servant steadies himself to tell the truth and Oedipus to hear it,

> SERVANT. Oh no, I'm right at the edge of telling the terrible truth!
> OEDIPUS. And I'm at the edge of hearing it, but hear it I must!
>   (1169–70),

this shattering climax is one of the defining moments of dramatic literature. One particularly heart-stabbing effect comes with Oedipus' empathy, even at this crisis of appalled realization, with the wretched mother who was driven to try to kill her child (1175). Yet is the reversal, the change of fortune, altogether a downward one from good to bad fortune as Aristotle believes it to be (*Poetics* 1453a)? I shall suggest at the end of this chapter that it is not.

To move on to the limitations of psychological readings of the play, Freud's identification of the Oedipus complex, his statement that it is 'the fate of all of us, perhaps, to direct our first sexual impulse towards our mother and our first hatred and our first murderous wish against our father', along with his subsequent comment that 'our dreams convince us that this is so', seem to find serendipitous support in Jocasta's remark that 'many men have bedded with their mother in dreams' (981–2); but in fact they are totally inappropriate to a man who certainly killed his father and married his mother, but only in complete ignorance of who they were. Devereux' equation of self-blinding with castration carries considerably more conviction, but pushes aside the play's far more obvious use of the themes of sight and blindness. The blind Teiresias can see the truth while the seeing Oedipus cannot. When he does, he blinds himself. As in *King Lear* (KENT. See better, Lear ...; GLOUCESTER (when blinded). I stumbled when I saw (1.1.158 and 4.1.19)), the ideas of sight and blindness work so effectively on the most obvious metaphorical level that it is surely a distraction to insist too much on further resonances.

If I raise objections to what strike me as over-schematic assessments of the play, this does not mean that I wish to problematize it. Indeed, what have struck many as its most obvious difficulties do not strike me as problematic at all. Teiresias' levelling of the charges of parricide and incest at Oedipus (457–60) corresponds so closely to the prophecy which the latter will say was given to him (791–3) that it seems to some incredible that he fails to make the connection. Yet it would surely be easy for the actor playing Oedipus to suggest here that he is simply blinded by the rage that possesses a number of Sophocles' heroes. Alternatively, if Oedipus remains rational, he *knows* he never met Laius and so Teiresias must be lying: nothing the seer says after claiming that Oedipus killed Laius can be taken at face value. Similarly Oedipus fails to take Jocasta's words in fully when she raises the subject of parricide at 720–2. However, an actor will have no difficulty in conveying the impression that Oedipus has been knocked sideways by her mention of the place where three roads meet (716). His recognition of the site of his multiple killings leaves him deaf to what follows. Other literal-minded objections – such as the pairing of the coincidences that (a) the servant who handed over the child should have been the one that got away from the murder of Laius and his retinue, and (b) the shepherd who received the child should have turned up as the messenger from Corinth – seem to confuse the drama's laws with the operations of statistical probability. Has a single member of a theatre audience given a moment's thought to either purported implausibility as the screw is turned in these scenes with their agonizing accumulation of tension?

Even the more general structural problems which I discussed above will perhaps evaporate if one can put aside the expectations of neat symmetry that have dogged the play – perhaps because of a tendency to view it as the world's first-ever detective story – and recognize its movement from the political to the personal, from the pollution of an entire land to that of a single family, from the *polis* (city) to the *oikos* (house). If this is indeed the better way to view to view the play, need we be surprised? After all, the cause of the land's pollution is its royal family with their sick saga of parricide and incest. Even though the play shifts from the world outside the *oikos* to the world within it, the play's religious emphasis, of course, does not abate. The pollution in the one is a mirror image of the pollution in the other.

We certainly begin in a civic context as the Priest of Zeus supplicates Oedipus with representatives of the young and old of the community (16–19) and the point is rammed home in the famous lines:

A walled city and a ship are nothing if they are empty of men living inside them. (56-7)

One of the main dramatic functions of Creon in the play seems to be to emphasize its civic dimension. Oedipus thinks he has been plotting with Teiresias to remove him from the kingship (385-7) and Creon tries to reassure his brother-in-law that he is altogether content politically (584-602). At the climax of their impassioned argument, Oedipus cries out, 'O city, city!' (629). The play's political dimension continues to be important at least until the ship of state metaphor in 922-3 but by now a concentration on the personal, on the family of Oedipus, is beginning to be felt. When the Servant who had exposed Oedipus as a baby arrives, the hero questions him not about the killing of Laius, the reason he was sent for, but about who he (Oedipus) is. He is seen more and more in relation to his dead father and his mother and after his blinding we find him expressing deep concern for his beloved daughters as he embraces them. His final words in the play are his appeal not to have them taken from his arms (1522). The barrenness of the land of Thebes has indeed been transferred to the wombs of the girls (1502). With the play's reflux from the large expanse of Thebes to the little – though dramatically immense – world of Oedipus' family, it is scarcely surprising that he now goes back into the house. We can appreciate all over again how consummately the play is constructed.

We sup full of horrors in *Oedipus the King* but it is, paradoxically, an exhilarating play. One reason for this may be its superb structure. Another may lie in the unsurpassed vitality of its poetry: the extraordinary, terrifying evocation of the plague (see, for example, the whole of the first chorus), the deluded outbursts, almost iambic arias, of Jocasta and Oedipus at 977-83 and 1076-85, and the wild, heady optimism of the chorus as they speculate on what they suppose to be Oedipus' divine parentage (1086-1109), all these make the pulse beat faster, the heart pound. The characterization is dazzling too: the spookily quiescent politician Creon who ends the play a curious compound of sensitivity and crass imperiousness; the agonized Teiresias, the prophet in an unwinnable situation who is tragically provoked to rage; the buffoonish Messenger from Corinth, whose eagerness to help has such disastrous consequences; the decent, sympathetic Servant with his futile tergiversations. The character of Jocasta is particularly well delineated. A commanding figure – she sorts out her husband / son in his row with Creon with a mother's intuition –, she is nevertheless a prey to insecurity. Trying so hard to be pious (911–23) – and we should remember that she tried to expose her son because of her total faith in Apollo's oracle (1175–6) – she strays dangerously close to blasphemy (977–83).

Towering above all the others like a damaged archangel (to adapt Charles Lamb's description of Coleridge) is Oedipus. A character of enormous energy and determination, he is impulsive, solipsistic and prone to rage. He cannot pause to take stock, he cannot brook frustration, he must rush ever onwards on his journey regardless of the consequences for those about him. His mission *is* crowned with success, he *does* bring everything to light. At a terrible cost to himself, he triumphs; and it is vital to Thebes and the impious *oikos* at its heart that he should do so. If Oedipus fails, the plague blasting the land and the pollution afflicting the royal house will remain unabated. Teiresias refuses to help, Creon has proved unavailing in the past (126–31), the Servant and Jocasta plead with him to leave the matter alone. And yet he insists remorselessly on carrying out Apollo's command (96–8) and tracking down the source of pollution. As we have seen, again and again he urges that it be expelled from the land. He is the one man with the drive and strength of character to save the city, as he has already proved by solving the riddle of the Sphinx. In addition, he has had the devotion of his people and surely the supportive love of his wife. He is a loving and caring father. This is a superbly detailed characterization of a monarch overwhelming in his dynamism and commanding huge admiration and respect.

Underpinning the action is the chorus of leading Theban noblemen (1223), perhaps the most authoritative of the choruses in Greek tragedy (649–72), certainly one of the least marginalized despite their old age (1111).[10] They will surely have some influence on audience opinion as they gradually move from total confidence in Oedipus, even when he is under fire (503–12), through increasing doubts until they finally wish that they had never seen or known him (1217–18 and 1348). They appear to adjudge him a hubristic tyrant (873). In a breath-taking passage, they sing that they would rather believe that the play's oracles are true – i.e. that a man should commit the ultimate sacrilege of killing his father and marrying his mother – than find the fabric of their religion rent asunder (897–902). If sacrilege triumphs, what value is there, they ask, in dancing in a religious ritual – which surely prompts the audience to think of the theatrical festival sacred to Dionysus in which they are dancing as they sing these lines (883–96). The old religion is terrifying but at least it deals in certainties and gives a framework for mortal life. The alternative is godless anarchy:

> The old oracles of Laius are dying, they are discarding them now, and nowhere is Apollo's honour plain and clear. The gods are disappearing. (906–10)

Indeed, the chorus' view of the play's action is a bleak one and that may seem highly appropriate to this terrible tale of parricide, incest and self-mutilation. Yet we in the audience may be able to see something that they, in their shuddering horror (1306), cannot. When they ask Oedipus which of the gods drove him to his self-blinding, he replies:

> It was Apollo, friends, Apollo who wrought these my terrible

sufferings. But the hand that struck my eyes was mine alone, the hand of wretched Oedipus. (1329–31)

Yes, it all goes back to Apollo, but Oedipus takes upon himself the responsibility for the fearful deed that he has committed. By doing so, he seems to have moved into a strange new world where the gods have no power to touch him:

Yet this much I know: no sickness nor anything else could have destroyed me. For I would never have been saved from death unless for something strange and terrible. (1455–7)

Pounded by his destiny, he refuses to be crushed. Under the pressure of extreme agony and misery, he remains indomitable. For the chorus he is a paradigm warning them to count nothing human happy (1195). At the same time he is also a paradigm of the invincible human spirit. In this strange and terrible world in which he now moves, he has transcended the worst the gods can do to him.

CHAPTER 6

ELECTRA

WILD JUSTICE

Sophocles' *Electra* is a blood-stained revenge play dealing with the words, deeds and visceral emotions of the ultimate dysfunctional family. So it may seem something of a paradox that it can prove so exhilarating in the theatre. This may be due to the strong characterization of the dramatis personae, so sharply etched on their entries, to the energy of the play's mainly confrontational episodes and to its fluent forward momentum. We may start with the bright light of the sun that has caused the birds to sing and the night to fail (17–19), but we soon find ourselves propelled, thrilled and horrified, through a dark, bloody tale of love, hate and murder.

I begin by singling out two dramatic effects that illustrate the consummate skill of the play's design. One comes when Clytemnestra has prayed to Apollo that her dream may foretell a good outcome for herself and her friends (644–56) and the old Tutor immediately enters with the false news of Orestes' death. It looks as if Apollo has granted her prayer, while Electra's hopes lie shattered. In reality, of course, the Tutor is here launching the successful plot on Clytemnestra's life and Electra will find grimly passionate satisfaction in its fulfilment. A second striking effect comes at the start of the following scene when Electra's sister Chrysothemis brings her joyous (and this time accurate) news of Orestes' return.

Electra, convinced that Orestes has died in a chariot race, refuses to believe her. In both of these scenes Sophocles' dramatic exploitation of his characters' states of ignorance and / or knowledge takes the breath away – and tugs at the heart strings. His use of irony is at its most expressive.

The fine craftsmanship of this relentlessly fast-moving play makes one of its features seem all the more disconcerting. I refer to the abruptness of its ending. The avengers are given no expressions of joyous triumph, Aegisthus is ushered into the palace and we are left with the chorus' final three lines asserting fulfilment. Many have felt it hard to find satisfying closure here. In addition, the virtuosity with which Sophocles unfolds the main action is reflected, to unsettling effect, in the illusory play within the play that Orestes so brilliantly stages to make his stratagem (outlined in the prologue (39–58)) unfold. This, of course, has to be deceptive – a bag of tricks – if it is to succeed, but it leads the spectator into a mire of confusion between illusion and reality. Greek audiences trusted tragic messengers, who describe events that have taken place away from the acting area. Thus there is nothing apart from the messenger's words to validate their truth. In this play, the Tutor communicates the false news of Orestes' death in the precise format of the messenger scenes of Greek tragedy, down to the standard crisp announcement, here made twice (673 and 676), of *what* has happened in advance of the full description of *how* it happened. With the verve and excitement of its narrative momentum and its wealth of visual and aural detail, his account of the hero's death in a chariot race obviously seems true to Electra, Clytemnestra and the chorus *and*, I would add, to the audience, even though they know at another level of their consciousness that it is false. The confusion between truth and illusion is further complicated by the metatheatrical nature of the narrative which shows an intensely involved audience (749–51) watching a scene of disaster in the hippodrome at Delphi, thus reflecting the two audiences, the one on stage and the other listening to the speech in the theatre of Dionysus at Athens. (Postmodernists call this effect *mise en abîme*.)

A similar situation arises in what has a strong claim to be considered the most heart-rending speech in Greek tragedy, that in which Electra mourns her (supposedly) dead brother as she holds the urn which she believes contains his ashes (1126–70). The depth and sincerity of her emotion, overwhelming enough to break the bounds of the iambic metre at 1160–2, are so obviously genuine that it becomes difficult not to believe in the genuineness of what she is mourning even as the living Orestes stands on stage. At one and the same time the spectators think that Orestes is dead and know that he isn't. To the extent that they cling to their awareness that Orestes is in fact still alive, they reflect on the appalling sorrow which his stratagem is causing Electra. This, of course, is a key element in what moves them. Orestes himself may recognize some of this when he determines to take the urn from her (1205ff.). It is too palpable a symbol of his false death. The shifting interplay between illusion and reality consistently denies the audience any settled response.

This kind of slippery terrain is famously explored by Shakespeare in the scene in *King Lear* in which Edgar leads his blind father Gloucester onto the unlocalized Jacobean stage and, in a lengthy speech replete with circumstantial detail, both visual and aural as in the Tutor's speech, describes the vertiginous Dover cliffs above which he claims they are standing (4.5.11ff.). This celebrated passage begins:

> Stand still. How fearful
> And dizzy 'tis to cast one's eyes so low!
> The crows and choughs that wing the midway air
> Show scarce so gross as beetles. Halfway down

Hangs one that gathers samphire, dreadful trade!
Methinks he seems no bigger than his head.

In fact, it is all an illusion: throwing himself over what he believes
to be the cliffs, Gloucester falls forward onto the stage. Yet Edgar
employs precisely the decriptive technique that creates location in
Elizabethan / Jacobean drama. The *Lear* audience would believe in
the cliffs, they would see them in their mind's eye. They would in
fact become far more real than the reality of the unlocalized stage,
and thus dramatic illusion would become profoundly subversive of
dramatic reality. Sophocles and Shakespeare here join hands across
the centuries.

At this point it may be helpful to discuss the extreme polarization
of critical views of Sophocles' *Electra*. On the one hand, this play,
in which a son, ardently urged on by his sister, murders his mother
in a revenge killing, is seen as an ethically problem-free zone. The
murders of Clytemnestra and Aegisthus are entirely justified and
there are no problems. This approach is most famously encapsulated
in Gilbert Murray's description of the work, based on Schlegel's
formulation, as 'a combination of matricide and good spirits'. On the
other hand, as the twentieth century progressed, critics, provoked
– like Aeschylus and Euripides in their treatments of the myth
– by the question of whether you can murder your mother and still
remain fundamentally innocent, increasingly tended to take a darker
view of the play, finding in it an undertow of disturbing elements.
A commonsense response to this divergence in critical views would
be to accept that, since they totally contradict each other, directors
and audiences have to settle for one of them and exclude the other.
A more nuanced response may, however, be available to us.

The combatants on this critical battlefield inevitably find
themselves privileging some passages or text and / or having
to 'explain away' others. Take, for example, the presentation of

Electra's mother Clytemnestra. She offers as a justification for her murder of her husband Agamemnon – not unreasonably, one might think – that he had killed their daughter Iphigenia (530–46). Jenny March, at present the leading exponent of the 'positive' view of the play, remarks that Sophocles 'allows Clytemnestra to make no mention of any love she may have borne her daughter'. 'It seems rather,' she adds, 'that Clytemnestra sees Iphigenia's death as an offence against herself and her rights of possession as a mother; she does not question the fact that a child should have died, but merely asks why *her* child.' Well, maybe. (In his prequel to the action of this play, *Iphigenia at Aulis*, Euripides enters with sensitive empathy into the emotions of Clytemnestra at this terrible juncture. Though she has so far proved the model wife (1157–65), she can see only too well that if Agamemnon kills Iphigenia, she will be nursing bitter feelings as she waits at home for the whole duration of the Trojan War (1171–84). In effect, he will transform her into a murderess.) March's somewhat chilling commentary on the mother, however, may perhaps invite the response that her daughter Electra is permitted to feel no emotion at all about her sister's murder. There is absolutely no mention of any love that she may have felt for her, merely an expression of the opinion that it was right to kill her. (Contrast Aeschylus' *Libation Bearers* where she *does* speak of her love for her pitilessly sacrificed sister (241–2).) If we are to judge Clytemnestra by what she does not say, we should surely accord the same treatment to Electra, especially since we actually see her behaving with such harshness to her surviving sister Chrysothemis on stage.

Another passage that 'positive' readers of the play have to come to terms with is that in which she reacts to the (in fact fictional) account of Orestes' death with a stab of maternal feeling:

CLYTEMNESTRA. O Zeus, what is this? Am I to call it

> fortunate, or terrible but profitable? It's a painful situation
> if I save my life at the cost of disaster for myself.
> TUTOR. Why are you so despondent, lady, at my news?
> CLYTEMNESTRA. Bearing a child is a strange thing, for even
> when you suffer bad treatment from them, you cannot hate
> your own children. (766–71)

Of these lines the superbly commonsensical A.J.A. Waldock remarks,
'Clytemnestra drops a tear – and notes her emotion with surprise.
It is only a passing pang, a reaction of some nerve of motherhood,
not quite atrophied even in her. She smothers it with no trouble.'
He could of course be right, but not necessarily. I find such attempts
to empty Clytemnestra's two sympathetic expressions of maternal
feeling of any real significance glib and superficial. Maurice Bowra
falls into the same kind of trap when he writes that 'it is clear
that all goodness has died ..., that she is irremediably corrupted, a
lost soul'. Yes, but what has made her so? No doubt she is an evil
woman. If it is true that she celebrates the murder of her husband
with monthly dances and rites, as Electra tells the chorus (278–81),
that is certainly repulsive. Yet there is much to be said on her side.
I return to the fact that Agamemnon had killed their daughter.
Electra feels that he had no choice (573–6) but freely concedes
that the sacrifice was necessitated by Agamemnon's hubris (569:
he let fall some boast). Why should Clytemnestra stay faithful to
the blood-stained killer of her child? Nobody actually comes out
with it and states that she would have killed the infant Orestes
if she could have got her hands on him, though it has to be said
that Electra comes pretty close to doing so at 601 and 1133. Since
Orestes will slaughter her – as of course he does – when he comes
back home, it is scarcely surprising that the news that he has died
tears her in two. It is clear that she gloats *not* over her son's death
but over Electra's frustration (791–803). Sophocles would surely

feel disconcerted that some scholars take words about her mother which he puts in the mouth of this most disaffected of daughters as literal statements of fact.

On the other hand, not many have been persuaded by the extreme 'negative' interpretation of 766–71 (the exchange between Clytemnestra and the Tutor quoted above) offered by Kells in his 1973 Cambridge edition. He sees this moment as 'the very centre of the play', constituting an 'enormous reversal in the stage action' with a 'far-reaching significance for the play's total meaning' since it is a now sympathetically transformed Clytemnestra who is to be horrifically murdered. Such a subjective reading would scarcely be worth quoting were it not a feature of a much-used modern edition of the play as well as an only too apt illustration of the interpretative confusion to which the present critical *aporia* has led us.

Indeed it may be that this very *aporia* is a vital guide to an appropriate interpretation of the play. It is at all events exactly what one would expect in a work in which, as we discussed at the outset, the interplay between truth and illusion is so deeply disorienting. In espousing an unclouded, optimistic view, Jenny March makes it clear that she has no quarrel with different interpretations of the play in modern productions but states that her concern is 'to focus on Sophocles' text'. There is perhaps a touch of hubris in the echo here of the harpsichordist Wanda Landowska's famous dictum, 'You play Bach your way, and I'll play him *his* way.' But, more importantly, what on earth does March's statement mean? Sophocles' *Electra* is a text that constantly deconstructs itself, most dazzlingly – and self-consciously – so in the extraordinary riddling scene in which Electra welcomes Aegisthus on his return. Every single thing that she says carries two meanings.

Two further examples of the volatile nature of the dramatic text may repay attention. Those who feel that the act of matricide problematizes the play will have to grapple with the fact that Apollo's oracle ordains it. One answer to this is that it may not have done so. Orestes did not ask Apollo *whether* he should take vengeance on his father's murderers but *how* he should do so (33–4). This point strikes a number of critics as so much sophistry; but the Greeks did care about this kind of thing: when Xenophon returned from consulting Apollo's oracle about going on a military expedition to Persia, Socrates criticized him for not first asking whether he should go or stay but making up his own mind and asking about the best way of going (Xenophon, *Anabasis* 3.1.6–7). March reminds us that 'the words of the oracle itself instruct Orestes to carry out "lawful killings" (36–7)'; but she neglects to say that we only hear what the oracle says through Orestes' lips. (Modern critics making this point would say that Sophocles *focalizes* the oracle through Orestes: his report reflects his own view.) If Sophocles had wanted to create a greater impression of objectivity, he could have made the Tutor quote the oracle. It is thus a perfectly respectable interpretation of the text to say that Orestes may be adding the word 'lawful' to the utterance of the oracle in order to convince himself that he is about to act justly. Corroboration can then be added by citing the notorious line which Orestes delivers after killing his mother: 'All is well in the house if Apollo prophesied well' (1424–5). It could be correct to take the word 'if' as meaning 'as sure as' (cf. 'if the Pope's a Catholic': i.e., of course Apollo prophesied well, and so naturally all is well); but it could possibly be more natural to assume that the word 'if' represents a straightforward 'if' and thus lends the line the strong implication of 'but what if he didn't prophesy well?'

Support for the latter reading may be offered by consideration of how the Athenians would have felt about Apollo's oracle at Delphi in the course of the Peloponnesian War. It appears, in fact, that they considered it to be biased in favour of their bitter enemies, the Spartans (Thucydides 1.118, 1.121 and 1.123; Plutarch, *De Pyth. or.* 29; Aristophanes, *Knights* 1059) and chose rather to consult the oracles of Thesprotia, Dodona and Ammon (Plutarch, *Nicias* 13; Pausanias 8.11.12). An Athenian audience might well have felt deeply suspicious of Apollo's guidance to Orestes. On the other hand, in a play set in a distant heroic age, it might have viewed the oracle as sacrosanct. The avenue that history ushers us along may in fact prove to be a cul-de-sac.

Even if one remains agnostic on that matter, a strong case can surely be made for seeing both these passages as truly ambivalent, each holding two possible meanings in an equivocal balance entirely characteristic of this play. In another area, this characteristic uncertainty lends an ominous aura to the proceedings. For his scheme to work, Orestes must pretend to be dead. Is this pretence of death a bad omen or isn't it (59–61)? Orestes first of all persuades himself that it is not. Later, as I have suggested, the Tutor, in his superbly circumstantial account of the chariot race, and Electra, in her poignant mourning over the urn, almost persuade us that he *is* dead. At 1210–11, when Electra talks of giving him burial, he tells her to avoid words of bad omen. Pretence and trickery are of course vital, but the constant talk of Orestes' death proves deeply unsettling, almost especially when Aegisthus assumes that it is Orestes' corpse that he sees on the stage. (In fact, it is Clytemnestra's.) And when Orestes so evidently fails to respond to Electra's ecstasy in their recognition scene, doggedly sticking to the iambic rhythm of the play's action scenes in contrast to her lyric outpourings, one may wonder whether his fearful duty to vengeance has killed off much of the vital spark within. It may be possible to view Orestes less as a gung-ho vengeful *ephebe* (the Athenian term for a young warrior) than as an animated spectre.

I hope I have said enough to indicate that in *Electra* language becomes a decidedly insecure index to the truth. Can I go on to suggest that we should not necessarily be looking for the critical certainties that scholars have been so eager to find in the play? After all, there are no stable landmarks in a quicksand. Through the play's prism of shifting viewpoints, it may be right to see Clytemnestra as *both* a woman deeply corroded by evil *and* a human being once possessed of powerful maternal instincts which are now largely atrophied because of what life has done to her. All the terrible things that Electra says about her mother can appear true from the daughter's perspective, many of them may be, within the terms of the play, objective facts – though it is no doubt impossible to say which would be and which wouldn't – but they do not not constitute a final judgement. Equally, it is unwise to take everything she says about Aegisthus as dramatic truth. Her detestation for him is, of course, altogether understandable but when he appears and is faced with death, he comes across not as a stage villain but as dignified and self-controlled.

To recognize the destabilizing factor inherent in the play is, I feel, to acknowledge the mastery of Sophocles' characterization more fully than both 'positive' and 'negative' readers who find themselves polarizing the dramatis personae into simplistic categories of good and bad. Since when have people in plays, let alone in real life, been so easily categorized? A recent attempt to 'defend' Electra has been based on the belief that the general view among ancient Greeks was that revenge was totally natural and unproblematic. This may or may not be the case.[11] However, even if it is, there remains the significant matter of what the act of revenge does to the avenger. The fury-driven Orestes of Aeschylus and Euripides is tragedy's most famous exemplar of the profound psychological damage inflicted on the avenger by a justified act of revenge. Hecuba, in the eponymous play of Euripides, is bestialized by it: she is indeed to be transformed into a dog (1265). In his history of the Peloponnesian War, Thucydides devastatingly portrays the escalation of terrible cruelty as real-life contemporaries of Sophocles hardened themselves to violence. It was surely this kind of awareness that made the dramatist cause his on-stage Electra to urge on her brother within the house to further, horrific brutality:

Strike twice as hard, if you have the strength. (1415)

Her final words show only too clearly the acid effect that loathing has had on an essentially loving character:

No, kill [Aegisthus] as quickly as you can and once you've killed him, put him out for the buriers it is fitting for him to meet with [i.e. carrion animals and birds], out of our sight – since for me this alone would free me from my past sufferings. (1487–90)

Earlier she conceded that her true self had been depraved by living with her mother in an atmosphere of hatred (616–21); and she has perhaps sought refuge in her idolization of her father, to some extent (no doubt) a figure of fantasy whose actual nature is briefly glimpsed when, as we have seen, we discover from her own lips that he uttered the blasphemous boast that necessitated his sacrifice of his daughter Iphigenia (569). Her capacity for love must be set against her harsh treatment of her sister Chrysothemis, an appealing and far from weak character who has made compromises but desires so intensely to be loyal to her. And yes, of course she is immoderate, as even the sympathetic chorus of Argive women points out (140). Yet what 'positive' critics apparently fail to realize is that such defects make Electra seem more human, more real. Not only do we sympathize with her as a victim of present and threatened abuse (191, 379–82 and 451; lines 1180–9 offer objective evidence of it), but we love her for her very capacity to love. The intensity of her grief over her brother is overwhelmingly moving (808–22, 1126–70) as is her outpouring of ecstasy at the moment of recognition (1225–87). This fleshed-out characterization is deeply affecting and the way in which she is ultimately reduced to an icon of hatred is profoundly tragic.

If we are correct in seeing ambivalence as a pervasive feature of the play, we may perhaps arrive at an interpretation of the chorus' concluding lines that responds both to the 'positive' and to the 'negative' readings of the play and can accommodate both of them at the same time: 'O offspring of Atreus,' they chant, 'after how many sufferings have you come through at last in freedom, brought to fulfilment by the present enterprise!' (1508–10) Vengeance will soon be complete and a world out of joint will be set right; there *is* cause for rejoicing. At the same time, the tendency of the play to destabilize, to deny a secure foothold, may be felt here too, exposing a too easy confidence, a certain glibness. And we may in fact hear that 'eternal note of sadness' that, according to Matthew Arnold, Sophocles heard on the Aegean, bringing to his mind 'the turbid ebb and flow of human misery'.[12] We may indeed feel that we have been denied a reassuring closure.

CHAPTER 7

PHILOCTETES

THE CURE ON LEMNOS

One of the most remarkable features of Sophocles' *Philoctetes* is the playwright's decision to make the eponymous hero so physically repellent. In the tragedy's opening speech, Odysseus tells us that he dumped him on the island of Lemnos because 'his foot was festering with a ravening sore' and 'shouting, yelling, he for ever distracted the whole fleet with his wild ill-omened cries' (7–11). We shall hear quite a few of these cries of agony in the play. Soon Neoptolemus spots Philoctetes' rags hung out to dry 'full of offensive discharge from his sore'. ('Ugh!' exclaims one of the translators [13] (38–9).) When an agonizing attack hits him, a 'boiling gush of blood oozes from the sores of his poisoned foot' (696–7). He tells us how 'the blood is gushing from the wound's depths and dripping red again' (783–4). And Neoptolemus says that 'a stream of blood from a vein has burst out black from his heel' (824–5). The Greek word for sickness (*nosos*) resonates throughout the play. Philoctetes stinks (876, 890–2 and 1031–2). He is the first to admit that it is disgusting to be with him. Nobody wants to take him home (310–11) and he suggests that Neoptolemus should stow him in the ship in the place where he will cause the least distress to his companions (473–4 and 481–3). Dressed in beast skins, he has become wild himself (226 and 1321). Yet despite all this, we surely admire him. This presentation of Philoctetes is all the more remarkable when we consider that after Euripides in his now-lost *Telephus* made his hero dress in rags in order to win a cure for a leg wound, he was mercilessly mocked by Aristophanes for his obsession with such tattered costumes (*Acharnians* 412–34 and *Frogs* 842, 1063–6). Why then should Sophocles escape the comic dramatist's ridicule? One answer to this may lie in the flinty integrity of his hero and the extraordinary range and visceral passion of his language. His unforgettable outburst at 927–62, with its astonishing modulations of tone, is among Greek tragedy's greatest gifts to an actor; and there is much else in the role to challenge the versatility and reach of the protagonist's technique. The power and intensity of it all effectively snuff out any opportunities for poking fun. Another factor may be that Philoctetes' repulsive sickness will – so we discover as the play nears its end – ultimately be cured at Troy (1333–4, 1378–9, 1424). Implicit in the sickness is the promise of health. (But Euripides' Telephus is cured too.) Yet another answer could be that it sets a challenge to the play's characters – how will they react to so repellent a figure? – and thus serves as a touchstone to illuminate their moral qualities, just as the way the suitors treat Odysseus in his beggar's disguise in the *Odyssey* shows up their degeneracy. The moments when Neoptolemus establishes physical contact with Philoctetes, the first as a pledge that he will not leave him (813), the second when he stops him from shooting Odysseus (1300–3) and the third as a literal support as he agrees to risk the ravaging of his country for his new-found friend (1403–7), are charged with enormous emotional force as they reveal his essential goodness. He does not recoil from touching the stinking cripple. He can penetrate the repulsive exterior and see his heroic heart.

Thus Philoctetes' condition is certainly grim but it also invites us to consider the possibility of a cure for him as well as offering a challenge to Neoptolemus which plays a crucial part in the moral education of this ephebe (the Athenian term for a young warrior).

This balance between the negative and the positive is reflected in the depiction of the island of Lemnos on which the play is set. Rocky and mountainous – it has its own volcano –, it is unpopulated (in contrast with Homer's Lemnos (*Iliad* 7.467–75) as well as the treatments of the story by Aeschylus and Euripides) and offers no good anchorage. An inhospitable location. Yet here Philoctetes lives in a user-friendly cave which, according to Odysseus, catches the sun in winter and is well ventilated in summer (17–19). Close by, there is a spring of drinking water and on the island grows the pain-killing herb which brings the damaged hero relief (44, 649–50 and 704–5). In the *Iliad*, which would have been well known to Sophocles' audience, Lemnos is the island where Sleep dwells (14.230–1). In our play, sleep brings to Philoctetes precious relief from his pain (766–7, 821–2, 827–32, 859 and 877–8). The ambiguous nature of the island is reflected by the cave's two entrances (16, 159 and 952) and the fact that Philoctetes says that it is both hot and frosty (1082); and the position of Lemnos right at the heart of the Aegean sea midway between Greece and Troy is surely significant. It is well located for voyages not only to Philoctetes' Oetean land and Neoptolemus' Scyros but also to Troy.

This ambivalence makes Sophocles' Lemnos the perfect location for the moral testing and education of its characters. Will they leave the island as good or bad men? Odysseus is revealed as utterly ineducable, his rotten cynicism appearing far more repulsive than Philoctetes' physical degradation, even if his Machiavellian approach is in fact the only realistic one. (It is startling to note that Dio Chrysostom, an ancient writer who had to hand Sophocles' play as well as the lost treatments of the story by Aeschylus and Euripides, found Sophocles' Odysseus 'more gentle and straightforward' than that of Euripides (52.16).) Odysseus and Philoctetes at one level fight a battle for Neoptolemus' soul like the good and bad angels in a medieval mystery play (971–2, 1007–12 and 1013–15). First, the youth is corrupted by the naked expediency of Odysseus revealed in such corrosive lines as:

> I know well, boy, that it is not in your nature to tell such [lies] nor to devise evil schemes. But since vctory is sweet, go through with it. We shall show ourselves honourable men another day. Now, give yourself to me and be shameless for a brief part of a day, and then for the rest of time be called the most pious of all mortals. (79–85)

But Neoptolemus' exposure to Philoctetes launches him on a voyage to self-discovery: his day on Lemnos will have led him from callow adolescence to an understanding of what male virtue really is. He repents (1270) and absorbs the older hero's gritty integrity into himself. We have already observed that, as the play nears its end, he is even willing to risk the ravaging of his own country in order to do what he believes to be right (1404–5). This all-male play (the only surviving one from the Greek corpus) is the ideal vehicle for the portrayal of an ephebe's initiation into true manhood.

Perhaps even Philoctetes wins through to a fuller understanding – with considerable assistance from Heracles. Some have felt that the latter's appearance as *deus ex machina* seems tacked on, with the sole aim of breaking the impasse the action has reached. Yet in my view it is the spring that releases Philoctetes, enabling him to do what something in him now very much wants to do. Through the close emotional bond he has formed with Neoptolemus, he has already learnt that no man, not even a solipsistic Sophoclean hero, is an island. After the young man's speech at 1314–47 urging him to go to Troy of his own free will, he exclaims:

> Alas, what am I to do? How can I go against the words of this man, who has advised me out of good will towards me? Well, am I to yield then? (1350–2)

At first the answer is no. He cannot endure the thought of consorting with the sons of Atreus and Odysseus (1354–7). Then his old comrade, the now deified Heracles, tells him go to Troy with Neoptolemus and he finds himself taking the advice of his *friends*, Heracles and the young man (1467).

Those who cannot see a psychological rightness in Philoctetes' change of heart may like to consider the first and greatest work of Greek literature, the *Iliad*. The word which begins this poem is 'wrath' (*menis*), the wrath that Achilles conceives against Agamemnon and then directs against Hector after the Trojan has killed Patroclus. He nurses his wrath for twenty-three out of the twenty-four books of the poem. Even after he has killed Hector, for twelve days he obsessively maltreats his corpse, provoking the disgust of most of the gods. He is trapped in a carapace of self-regarding and inflexible emotion every bit as surely as Philoctetes. Yet when Thetis comes down from Olympus to tell him that the gods are angry with him and that he should release Hector's body, he agrees in just two lines (24.139–40). He finds that the wrath has evaporated. It is the goddess' visit that has caused this to happen but it is equally the case that he must have been emotionally ready to listen to her exhortation. So it is, I feel, with Philoctetes.

There is surely a fondness in the wonderfully unsentimental lyrics with which he bids farewell to Lemnos. He has come to terms with his past and discovered that he has a future.

Come then, let me call upon the land as I leave. Farewell, O cave that watched along with me, and you nymphs of the water-meadows, and the strong crashing of the sea on the headland, where often my head was drenched in a corner of the cave by the south wind's blasts, and you hill of Hermes which often sent me a groan echoing my voice in my storms of distress. And now, O springs and Lycian fountain, I am leaving you,

I am now leaving you, though I had never thought that this would happen. Farewell, o land of Lemnos surrounded by the sea, and send me on a safe voyage which I cannot complain of, where great Fate is taking me and *the advice of my friends* and [Zeus,] the all-subduing god who has brought these things to fulfilment. (1452–68: my italics)

Psychologically he is cured while still on the island. And this particular island is an appropriate setting for a cure; for Hephaestus, referred to in the play at line 987, recounts in the *Iliad* (1.589–94) how, when he was thrown out of heaven by Zeus, he landed on Lemnos – there was little life in him – and there the inhabitants of the island took care of him. Sophocles' uninhabited island cannot offer Philoctetes a physical cure – in Euripides' play at least one islander looks after the crippled hero – but that will follow at Troy.

Two millennia later, in *The Tempest*, Shakespeare used a desert island in the same kind of way as a setting for his characters' education and self-discovery. (Interestingly enough, it is one of the only two of his plays that limit their action to a single day as most Greek tragedies, including *Philoctetes* (83 and 480), do.) 'In a poor isle,' one of the characters exclaims near the end, 'all of us [have found] ourselves' (5.1.215). And Prospero's rough but benevolent magic makes him an equivalent of Sophocles' Heracles. In fact, not all of *The Tempest*'s characters can be included in the happy ending but for most of the older generation the wounds of the past have been healed and the young have been educated to face the world away from the island. So in *Philoctetes* Odysseus cannot progress beyond the prison of his mean-spirited cynicism and, in any case, is humiliated dramatically by his jack-in-the-box reappearance at 1293 which could easily be played for comedy. Philoctetes and Neoptolemus, however, have been transformed and enriched. When they leave the island, they have found themselves, and possibly it is in the generosity of their new, cured identities that true heroism, as this play defines it, lies.

Yet Sophocles disconcertingly subverts the happy ending when he causes Heracles to exhort Philoctetes and Neoptolemus to show piety at Troy:

> But take heed of this – when you sack the land, respect the things of the gods. (1440–1)

These words would have activated in the Greek audience the recollection that, according to the epic tradition, on the night when Troy was sacked Neoptolemus in fact behaved with appalling sacrilege, slaughtering King Priam at Zeus' altar.[14] It seems that the audience is being asked to contemplate the fragility of the education he has experienced during his day on Lemnos. He has learned the arts of honour and friendship. Soon he will discover the brute within himself. But then they are going to the war and war is a brutish business. In Sophocles' refusal to give us a fully satisfying closure we see the alarmingly clear-eyed realism of a great dramatist.

CHAPTER 8

OEDIPUS AT COLONUS
THE JOURNEY'S END

A famous and no doubt apocryphal anecdote tells how Sophocles, at the age of around 90, was prosecuted by his sons on the grounds that he was incapable of managing his affairs. The dramatist was then at work on *Oedipus at Colonus* and his response was to recite the wonderfully evocative chorus in praise of the play's location, his own birthplace (668–719), and then to inquire whether the lines were suggestive of imbecility. He was acquitted and left the court amid ecstatic applause, as if from a theatre in which he had triumphed (Cicero, *De Senectute* 7.22 and Plutarch, *Moralia* 785B).

It's a good story, touching in its portrayal of an ageing playwright of evergreen genius routing his opponents with yet another dramatic triumph; but it's an unsettling one too, showing a father at loggerheads with his sons in a public forum. It brings only too readily to mind the horrific curses that Oedipus unleashes upon his sons in the play which Sophocles was supposedly working on (421–7, 789–90 and 1370–96), as well as the appalling treatment he has received from those sons, as Oedipus repeatedly insists and Polyneices readily admits (441–4, 591, 599–600 and 1265–6). Certainly *OC* does, up to a point, usher us into a *Lear*-like world where a father is at odds with his children. In one of the bleakest passages in Greek literature the chorus declare:

Not to be born is to be prized above all else. But when a man has been born, by far the next best thing is to go to where he has come from as quickly as possible. For when he has let youth with its light follies pass by, what blow of fortune, fraught with toil, does not afflict him? What suffering does not beset him? Envy, factions, strife, battles and killings. And finally old age falls to his lot, abhorred, weak, unsociable, friendless, with which dwell all woes upon woes. (1224–38)

'All dark and comfortless' indeed (*King Lear*, 3.7.83).

Yet it would surely be a serious mistake to allow the anecdote with which we began to tempt us to so bleak a view of the play as a whole. For, in total contrast, it repeatedly insists on the primacy of *love*. This comes across most strikingly in the extraordinarily loving relationship between Oedipus and his daughters, his utterly devoted and constant companion Antigone who has given up her chances of marriage to look after him (750–2) and the perhaps more superficial but certainly extremely loyal Ismene. The stage action twice arranges them in loving family tableaux (329–30 and 1104–14) and the Messenger tells us that these are replicated off-stage (1611 and 1620–1). Love is deeply woven into the fabric of their speech to each other (173, 201, 324–5, 332–3, 1104–6, 1108 and 1697–1703), finding its supreme expression in two utterances from the lips of Oedipus. He speaks the first as he embraces his daughters:

I hold what I love the best, and, if I were to die, I would not be utterly wretched since you two stand beside me. (1110–11)

The second comes from his final speech to his daughters, quoted by the Messenger:

Yet one little word frees you from all your toils. No man in the world loved you more than I did. (1615–18)

The 'one little word' is surely 'love'.

His deeply loving nature also finds expression in his feelings towards Theseus, who not for the first time in Attic drama (one thinks of his role in Euripides' *Suppliant Women* and *Heracles*) proves an exemplar of ideal Athenian behaviour towards a person or people in desperate need. Theseus' great-hearted awareness of shared humanity is conveyed most explicitly in the ringing declaration of 560–8 which concludes with the noble assertion:

> So never would I turn away from a stranger reduced to nothing
> as you are now or refuse to help to save him. For I know well
> that I am a man and that when tomorrow comes my portion is
> no greater than yours. (565–8)

Oedipus responds impressively to the Athenian king's generous display of *xeniā* (the operations of the guest / host relationship), showing a full understanding of its summons to reciprocity. Indeed, his attitude to the king verges on hero-worship (642, 1042–3, 1121–4 and 1496–8) and he venerates the king's city too as the champion of the weak (260–2 and 1124–9). He bonds movingly with the chorus of old men of Colonus, a strong relationship validated by the fact that it was initially so hard-won. Their unaffected tribute to him addressed to Theseus at 1014–15 carries considerable weight:

> The stranger is a good man, my king. His misfortunes are
> disastrous but they deserve our assistance.

This is indeed a good man and good people can relate to him. Love far predominates over hate in his make-up.

It is surely easy to regard him in a sympathetic light. His blindness, presumably ever evident from his mask and harped upon so repeatedly in the text, evokes pathos, as does his costume, memorably depicted by Polyneices in his description of his father at 1257–61:

... cast out here, dressed in clothes like these, the hateful filth of which has dwelt for so long an age with the old man, blighting his body, and on his sightless head his uncombed hair flutters in the wind.

In his dealings with those he loves or has no reason to hate he can seem diffident and humble, timid even (12–13, 21, 113–15, 170–3, 188–91, 203–16 and 465). He lays claim to his basic innocence over his killing of his father and marriage to his mother on three occasions (266–74, 521–48 and 962–99), surely betraying by his urgency an underlying insecurity which emerges not only in his formulation at 966–8 –

Take me by myself [apart from my ancestors], and you would find no sin to censure me for, in requital for which I sinned against myself and my family –

but also in his refusal to touch Theseus because of his own sense of pollution despite his belief that he is innocent:

Stretch out your right hand to me, O king, so that I may touch it and, if it is lawful, I may kiss your cheek. But what am I saying? In my wretchedness, how could I wish you to touch a man in whom every stain of evil has made its home? I would not wish you to do this, and I shall not allow you do so. (1130–5)

He shows flexibility in agreeing to see his son Polyneices in response to Antigone's persuasion (1181–1205) and Theseus' religious sensibility (1179–80, 1182–3 and 1348–51). In one of the play's most memorable speeches, in which the great poetry surges forth (607–23), he shows a greater awareness of flux of human affairs than the politically alert king of Athens.

These warmly human, sympathetic traits vanish, of course, when Oedipus is confronted with characters he despises or hates. In an effective dramatic coup, Sophocles causes Ismene to inform Oedipus – and the audience – of what the Thebans really intend to do with him before Creon weaves his tapestry of lies. They want to keep him just outside their borders so that his tomb will be easily accessible to them (399–402). Thus, when Creon appears and speaks with apparently sweet reason, we can detect his hypocrisy as thoroughly as Oedipus (728–60). His fraudulence is further revealed when we discover that he had kidnapped Ismene before he arrived. Later he threatens to snatch off Antigone (818–19) and does so. If both the Attic chorus and the king of Athens accuse him of outrage and he accepts the charge (883 and 1029), it is surely hard to find fault with Oedipus when he treats him with a combination of rage and scorn. Creon and Oedipus are the two old men among the protagonists – the former is the latter's uncle – but, unlike the nephew, who wishes to make his presence in Attica a blessing, the uncle has been reduced by his years to a state of ultimately ineffective folly, as Theseus observes (930–1). Even so, he imparts a real sense of menace to the play. He has troops with him (826–7) and there will be a battle before Theseus and his men rescue Oedipus' daughters. On the last count, however, he proves to be a bullying fraud, decidedly overparted as the tragedy's Machiavel.

If it is impossible to waste any tears on Creon, it is hard not to be chilled as well as harrowed by Oedipus' treatment of his son Polyneices. It is certainly true that the father sensationally fails to live up to the idea of parenthood enunciated so uncompromisingly by Antigone at 1189–91:

You are his father; so even if he were to commit the most impious and extreme wrongs against you, my father, it is not lawful for you to wrong him in return.

But at this point Sophocles is surely wishing us to think of his earlier play *Antigone*, in which the heroine makes the ultimate sacrifice of her life for her brutal and impious brother. Oedipus' strong sense of reciprocity blocks him off from his daughter's unconditional view of love (though one should note that in her case in *Antigone* it is directed exclusively towards a single individual when he is a corpse), but this does not brand him as harshly inflexible. He simply sees things as they are. We can trust him in both his hatred and in his love because they both relate to actual human behaviour. They are authentic emotions.

In any case, he first tries very hard to avoid a meeting with his son, only embarking upon it because of the passionate urging of his daughter and the will of Theseus. Neither Polyneices nor Antigone disputes the fact that the son drove the father into his destitute exile (1354–59). We have already noted Polyneices' acceptance of responsibility for his father's appalling state (1265–6). It was he who violated the contract between father and son. Now he has been driven out of Thebes with the people's assent (1298). Even if we can believe that he wishes to establish Oedipus in his own house (1342), it is only too evident that his father is essentially a pawn in a dynastic game. The chorus' comment after he has spoken makes it clear that, in their view, his appeal simply hasn't worked (1346–7).

Now there follows Oedipus' great speech cursing his son. It unfolds with a terrible, white-hot intensity unsurpassed in Greek tragedy and will inevitably appal an audience. Yet what is Polyneices' response? Though he knows that his expedition against Thebes is doomed, he refuses Antigone's pleas to turn his army back (1416–18). He will lead a huge force – he has punctiliously itemized its seven leaders in 1313–25 – to certain destruction because he is unwilling to be laughed at (1422–3). He will not even warn his followers:

> I shall not even announce bad news, for it is a good leader's job to tell the better news and not the worse. (1429–30 – cf. 1402–4)

In addition, he urges his sisters to give him burial (1410) in a course of action that we know will lead Antigone to her death. Indeed, our awareness of this causes his parting prayer, that his sisters may never meet with ill fortune (1445–6), to strike a chill to the heart. What deal could realistically be struck with such a man? An ancient Greek audience would have fully understood Oedipus' view of himself as a blessing to his friends and a curse to his enemies (92–3 and 459–60). The play's terrifying passions, so unflinchingly and powerfully laid bare to our hearts and minds, could well lead a modern audience to share that understanding.

This maelstrom of emotions, some of them loving, some of them violent, all of them passionate, has played itself out on a single day, the last one of Oedipus' long life. This is the place, this is the time, this is the moment (45–6, 86–91, 94–5, 101–3, 1540–1, 1626–8). But we are dealing in far more than temporal or spatial definitions. When Oedipus comes to the grove of the Furies at Colonus, he has reached his journey's end in dramatic terms too. In a series of a momentous concealed stage directions (stage directions that can be inferred from the text), the thunder sounds (1456, 1462–3, 1478–9: cf. 1606). Thereupon Oedipus summons Theseus and goes with Antigone, Ismene and the king into the grove of the Dread Goddesses [the Eumenides].[15] Inspired by an unseen power that calls him, he is no longer dependent on his daughters and he guides his followers towards the place where he will at last find rest (1542–6).

His death will prove a blessing not only for him but for others. What was forecast in 88–95 has now come to pass. In those lines Oedipus said that Phoebus

spoke of this as a rest for me after a long time, after I had come to my goal in a land where I should find a seat of the Dread Goddesses and a hospitable place, and he said that there I should bring my wretched life to an end, bringing benefits because I had dwelt there to those who received me but ruin to those who sent me away, who drove me out. And he communicated to me that signs of these things would come, either an earthquake or thunder or Zeus' lightning.

We cannot quite say that, as Oedipus finds rest, so does the play. The horrific ruin of his sons remains to be played out at Thebes and the end of the tragedy looks forward apprehensively to what may happen there (1769–72). However, there is a fulfilling benediction upon Athens, a blessing which will pass from one generation to another, from the presence there of the dead Oedipus, as the play so insistently drives home.[16] The wondrous passing of Oedipus is clouded in mystery for us and for all of the play's characters except Theseus but its miraculously benign significance is left in no doubt. The greatly loving hero is greatly beneficent in death.

AFTERLIFE

Ajax: the first Cambridge Greek play[17]

In 1880 Aeschylus' *Agamemnon* was produced at Balliol College, Oxford. Hard on its heels in 1881 came a Harvard *Oedipus the King*, then Euripides' *Alcestis* at Bradfield College, a school in Berkshire UK, early in 1882. The time seemed ripe for a Greek tragedy at Cambridge and – in accord with the 'cometh the hour, cometh the man' principle – a young graduate of Columbia and Heidelberg universities called Charles Waldstein, who had arrived in Cambridge in 1880 to be the first lecturer in classical archaeology there, found himself agreeing to direct Sophocles' *Ajax*. This reached the stage in late November 1882. The Cambridge *Daily News* remarked wryly that 'the public will doubtless be glad to see a confirmation of its fixed idea that Cambridge is generally behind the rest of the world; but if we are last in the field it will probably be allowed that in some respects the representation of the *Ajax* is more perfect than any that have preceded it'. However that may have been, it launched what has proved to be the most vigorous English tradition of performances of Greek tragedy and comedy.

The play was put on in a barn-like structure between Emmanuel College and the University Arms called St Andrew's Hall. It had once been a skating rink and could accommodate a sizeable audience, 'nearly 2,000 spectators at a pinch' according to the *Daily Telegraph*. The four performances (November 29, 30, December 1, 2) were extremely well attended, proved a financial success and met with an enthusiastic response. After one of them there was even a call for the 'Author' – attributed to one of the undergraduates present by the *Times* correspondent, who went on to say, 'It is somewhat characteristic [presumably of undergraduate behaviour] that, notwithstanding the proximity of Girton and Newnham [the two women's colleges], almost the only line applauded on its own merits' was 'Woman, silence is an adornment for women' (293). It was an all-male staging, women not being allowed to take part until they became full members of the university in 1948,[18] though in fact Mr A.R. Macklin, the actor playing Tecmessa, the single female part, won the most universal plaudits from the press. Much enthusiastic praise was showered on Mr J.K. Stephen, an appropriately beefy, strong-featured Ajax. Sadly, a few years later, this cousin of Virginia Woolf was to follow the character he impersonated in going mad himself. One author even alleged that he was Jack the Ripper!

In his Preface to the Greek text with R.C. Jebb's facing translation specially published for this production, Waldstein made it clear that, with regard to the stage decoration, scenery and costumes, 'an attempt [had] been made to bring the whole as near as possible to the time of Sophocles'. The critic of the *Daily News* felt that the attempt had proved successful. 'The stage itself,' he reported, 'is constructed with strict regard to archaeological propriety. The thymele [altar of Dionysus] in the centre of the orchestra is taken from the extant one in the theatre of Dionysius [*sic*] at Athens. The proscenium represents the front of the stage of a Greek theatre ... The effect of the whole is very beautiful.' Indeed, despite reservations about the proscenium from the *Academy* critic, the pencil jotting by Robert Farren reproduced as our frontispiece suggests an impressive degree of truth to ancient Greek staging.

The most obvious exception to this is, of course, the detailed painting of the backdrop, a feature entirely characteristic of the

Victorian theatre. There were in fact two sets for the production. The one illustrated in the jotting is the second one, 'A desolate place on the shore near the Grecian Camp.' The first, 'Shore of the Hellespont: the Grecian Camp before Troy', was even more naturalistic. As the *Daily News* described it, 'On the left is the portal of the hut of Ajax, closed by a curtain; on the right are the prows of the Greek ships, anchored in Archaic fashion to large stones. In front is the sea, rippling and blue in the morning light, and in the distance is the broken coast beyond the Hellespont.' Aristotle said that Sophocles invented scene-painting (*Poetics* 1449a), but this degree of detail would have been pushing things! Though the sets were fine, there was a certain amateurism about some features of the staging. The *Athenaeum* felt that 'the armour, and especially the shield of Ajax ... might ... have looked rather less flimsy'; and *The Times* pronounced that the bush 'behind which Ajax fell on his sword was wanting in the appearance of solidity, "too evidently in two dimensions," a Senior Wrangler [a top Cambridge mathematician] whispered'.

The chorus, that notorious stumbling-block in modern productions of Greek tragedy, numbered an authentic fifteen and won general approval. Percy Gardner in the *Academy* wrote, 'In spite of a few drawbacks, such as the awkwardness of arrangement of the sheep-skins worn by some of the Salaminian sailors, they looked, with their black beards and brown limbs, as rough-and-ready a set of sea-rovers as a man might find between Sicily and Cyprus. Their motions consisted, it is true, of not much more than marching up and down their little orchestra ...' From production photographs, their gestures look rather stagey and stiff. The critic of the *Daily News*, however, meditating on which of the odes he liked best, judged that 'the most striking was perhaps that in which the chorus rejoices in the belief that Ajax has renounced his project [to kill himself]. A rhythmic dance, with more elaborate movements and swaying of the hands, was introduced – a bold experiment justified by complete success.' There was also an interesting attempt to convey a wide age-group. Comparing them with the chorus in the Oxford *Agamemnon*, *The Times* drew attention to an evident advantage in *Ajax* – 'the Argives in [*Agamemnon*] are all elders, and one Argive elder looks very much like another, whereas the trusty followers of Ajax are of all ages, from "able-bodied seamen" to venerable old men who must at least be steersmen ...' This diversity of ages was a clear challenge to the concept of a totally uniform chorus and could well have been what Sophocles wanted. At all events, it seems to have worked in 1882.

Sir George Macfarren's music, directed by Charles Villiers Stanford, consisted of an orchestral prelude, four unison choruses with instrumental accompaniment, the last preceded by a funeral march, and an interlude introducing the second scene. 'The work is full of charming melody,' remarked the *Athenaeum*, 'and the unison choruses are so tastefully accompanied by the orchestra as never to become monotonous.' Whether charm and tastefulness are qualities that should be allowed admission to this particular play can be seriously questioned. As Philip Radcliffe, himself the composer for four productions of the Cambridge Greek play in the 1960s and 70s, observes, the music, 'apart from one mildly modal chorus, is very Mendelssohnian, and one could almost have expected Elijah [from Mendelssohn's famous oratorio] to appear on the stage'. The musical aspect of the tradition gained in dynamism as the years went by, perhaps reaching its apogee in 1909 with Ralph Vaughan Williams' music for Aristophanes' *Wasps*, a score that comes across as evergreen to this day.

The Greek was spoken in what we would now call the 'unreformed' pronunciation. This was especially regrettable in Cambridge, a university in which serious attempts had been made to establish the pronunciation of classical Greek in the sixteenth century. However, this had become hopelessly dislocated when soon afterwards the

Middle English vowel system shifted to that of modern English (in the so-called Great English Vowel Shift). Thus the cast, like all their successors until the 1950s when a systematic attempt was made to use the reformed pronunciation, were condemned to vocalizing sounds that *The Times* dubbed 'barbarous'. It would have been the same anywhere in England in 1882; so the *Vanity Fair* critic may have been unreasonable, even if accurate, when he declared his opinion that 'the Cambridge pronunciation of Greek is simply atrocious'. He goes on to say, rather more tellingly, that, however atrocious the pronunciation may be, 'the fashion in which with rare exception,[19] the University actors deliver themselves of poetic lines is worse. The majority of the lines in the tragedy were delivered in a sing-song, irritating, monotonous fashion ... The actors did not seem to *feel* the author's beautiful words; they simply *scanned* them, hopping from iambic to iambic ... Why on earth should not an actor speaking Greek give the passion and sense of the passage, and, while recognizing the metre, not emphasize it as if he were a schoolboy repeating a hardly-learned lesson? We do not scan Shakespeare, why scan Sophocles?' This tendency remains a serious bugbear but things have got better over the years. I am delighted to be able to report that the 2004 Cambridge play, *Oedipus the King*, was generally exemplary in this respect.

Let us finally consider the question of why the Cambridge Greek play should matter.

An article in *The Times* of the day before the first performance of *Ajax* expressed a high-Victorian point of view: 'In poring over and analyzing piecemeal the language of the Greek drama, we are too often blind to the spirit which inspires the language. The desire is strong with the student to see how the play, which he has been accustomed to use merely as a quarry whence to draw materials for his iambic verse, will appear, when subjected to the ordeal of scenic represen-tation, the test of a real play.' The essentially linguistic diet foisted on schoolchildren and undergraduates in the pre-1970s English system of classical education, with its enormous concentration (for males at least) on the composition of Greek and Latin prose and verse, was for the vast majority of its recipients a profoundly philistine and numbing experience. Regular performances of these ancient Greek masterpieces can regularly show that they work in the theatre, that they live, that they are life-enhancing. As Professor Jebb wrote of the *Ajax* production, 'The performance seemed to me very beautiful and very impressive. I felt I had never understood the play before.'[20] In one of his great Sophocles editions, he expressed his feeling that 'a new life has been breathed into the modern study of the Greek drama'. In another he referred to the Cambridge *Ajax* as 'to me a new revelation of meaning and power'. Everyone who is interested in the ancient theatre knows exactly what he means. Now that all of us, whether or not we know Greek, have discovered that we are actually allowed to appreciate these great works as drama, we understand more fully that the living theatre is the right place to study them.

Martin Crimp's *Cruel and Tender*

Martin Crimp's *Cruel and Tender*, his adaptation of *Women of Trachis*, grew out of his dicussions with the celebrated Swiss theatre and opera director Luc Bondy. What might Sophocles' play look like today? How could the ancient pattern be used to cut a play from the material of contemporary life? The resulting drama was performed in London, Chichester, Vienna, Recklinghausen, Paris, Villeurbaune and Zagreb in 2004. A compelling production, it was very well received; and the play seems likely to last.

It is certainly a convincing reconstruction of the ancient tragedy. We find some of Sophocles' imagery adapted to telling effect, as in the simile:

the father ...
only sees this child at distant intervals
like a farmer inspecting a crop
in a remote field. (2:[21] cf. Sophocles 31–3)

Crimp supplies his own equivalent of the original female chorus, consisting of the Beautician, the Physiotherapist and (at times) the Housekeeper. If their scenes smack of light relief, inhabiting a very different world from that of Sophocles' chorus with the range, depth and power of their poetry, two Billie Holiday songs ('My Man' and 'I Can't Give You Anything But Love') sound a note of raw passion. They are especially telling in that Holiday was notoriously a classic victim of abuse, both from others and from herself. Amelia, Crimp's Deianeira figure, begins and ends her role with the assertion that she is not willing to play the part of a victim (1 and 46). The naked emotionalism, so charged with vulnerability, of Holiday's singing is one of the factors that expose this as self-deluding bravado.

Crimp reproduces Iole's silence and Deianeira's initial sympathy with her in Amelia's first scene with Laela (the Iole equivalent). Much is made of Deianaira's famous remark about two women under one blanket (539–40: cf. pp. 27, 62 and 67). And the Messenger's exposure of Lichas' deception is faithfully mirrored in Richard's showing up of the slick, wheeler-dealing politician Jonathan. Richard makes his entry holding a bouquet of flowers (8). This echoes the flower imagery which conveys Deianeira's fading beauty and the bloom of Iole's youth (Sophocles 547–9). There is a foreboding intertextual message here: the *flores para los muertos* ('flowers for the dead') from Tennessee Williams' *A Streetcar named Desire* are surely evoked, as they are in Edward Albee's study of marital desperation, *Who's Afraid of Virginia Woolf?* When Crimp's chorus 'fill the room with flowers' to welcome the General home (33), the effect is decidedly more ironical than cheering.

No doubt inevitably, the most powerful evocations of Sophocles'
play convey the horrific action of the chemical (chillingly dubbed
'Humane') that destroys the general, in such grisly passages as:

> And there's this thing on his back, Mum – no – not on his back
> but under it – this thing under his skin – like an animal under
> his skin – it's crawling – it's crawling under his skin – like an
> animal, Mum, trying to slide out from underneath – which
> is the chemical – the animal under the skin – the pain – the
> chemical ... And when he turns round it's his eyes – it's worked
> its way up his spine and into his eyes – he's got these eyes like
> a cat in the sun – pin-point eyes – he isn't human, Mum – that's
> what you and your friend have done to him ... (40)

The spareness and incoherence of the writing here are supremely
expressive.

The General is brilliantly conceived as a Heracles for our times.
Through this deeply alarming figure, Crimp explores the frightening
ambivalence of the terrifying leaders who make war on terror. Iraq
cannot be far from the audience's thoughts. Addressing his son with
proud self-assertion, he lays claim to a civilizing mission, merging
his own identity with that of Heracles, the performer of labours,
even making use of ancient Greek:

>   ... I have purified the world for you.
> I have burnt terror out of the world for people like you ...
> So don't you talk to me about crimes
> because for every head I have ever severed
> two have grown in their place
> and I have had to cut and to cut and to cut
> to burn and to cut to purify the world –
> understand me?
> (*softly*) I killed the Nemean lion

oh yes –
with these hands – with these hands –
and the dog
the dog with the three heads
I collected it from hell in front of the cameras
I have visited the dead in front of the cameras –
Remember?
(Points to himself proudly.) Kallinikos. Kallinikos.
(57–8)

Kallinikos is a Greek epithet for Heracles meaning 'glorious conqueror'.

His claims to a civilizing achievement have been subverted by the war crimes to which he has been driven by his lust for Laela:

... he wants this girl so much – so much – he is so – what's the word? – inflamed – he is so – that's right – inflamed – that in order to take this girl from her father he is prepared to murder not just the father, but the inhabitants of an entire city ...
(18)

That is a shattering retrospective commentary on Heracles' sacking of Oechalia in *Women of Trachis*.

This unflinching portrait finds powerful expression in its stage representation. When he first appeared in the original production, the General was more or less naked, his privates visible, a catheter attached to his penis. Here surely we have the naked 'thing itself' from Act 3 of *King Lear* which I used as a point of reference for Sophocles' play in my earlier discussion. This repulsive, chemical-maddened figure represents a grim challenge to the audience – is this what we do to our warriors? – as well as, of course, to his son James (the Hyllus equivalent).

Crimp is particularly successful with this characteriziation. For the young man, the action of the play is a rite of passage as he grows from a lay-about adolescent to a man who can establish a relationship of some kind with his terrifying father. In an uneasy, entirely convincing scene he manages to hold his hand, which he had not been able to bring himself to do earlier (cf. 40 and 61). He agrees to 'talk to the doctors' about facilitating his death (60) and seemingly takes on the responsibility for Laela and her son (final stage direction). Crimp brings Hyllus' obedience to his father into the modern world and makes it totally plausible.

The playwright appears to depart most radically from his Sophoclean original in his portrayal of Amelia, who comes across as far more feisty, gutsy and overtly emotional than Sophocles' Deianeira. Yet perhaps this brash self-assertion is a front covering a fundamentally Deianeira-like insecurity. Certainly it crumbles before her suicide; and her final claim (which, as we have seen, looks back to her first speech) that she is not willing to play the victim rings out hollowly. Possibly Crimp's and Sophocles' conceptions of the character are not so far apart after all.

Crimp's play is full of pain and desperation but the two central characters, Amelia and the General, have a certain stature, even grandeur, amid the horror; and it may be that Laela's reading at the end of the play from Hesiod's description of the people of iron who will cause Shame and Truth to abandon the earth, is too uncompromisingly negative to prove a just summation of the world of *Cruel and Tender*. As James walks on at the conclusion with the boy (the son of Laela and his father) in his arms, the final thought is of a new generation and a better future. The idea of a new generation, of course, reflects the emphasis near the end of *Women of Trachis* on Heracles' command to Hyllus to marry Iole: they, as the audience would have known, were ancestors of the Heraclidae (the descendants of Heracles). But the suggestion of a better future is not something that I myself am able to find in Sophocles' play.

However, Crimp's adaptation offers so true and compelling a reading of the original as almost to persuade me that it is there.

Jean Anouilh's *Antigone*

During the middle decades of the twentieth century Greek tragedy became an important feature of the French theatre: the ancient plays were recycled by such figures as Jean Cocteau, André Gide, Jean Giraudoux, Jean Anouilh and Jean-Paul Sartre. The following words of T.S. Eliot about this kind of exploitation of Greek myth are taken from a 1923 review of James Joyce's *Ulysses* (published in *The Dial* in November of that year) but they can be applied equally well to the French dramatists. Such use of myth, Eliot says, 'is simply a way of controlling, or ordering, or giving a shape and significance to the immense panorama of futility and anarchy which is contemporary history'. One of the most durable of these works, as well as by far the closest to its source, is Anouilh's adaptation of Sophocles' *Antigone*. The play opened and had a highly successful run in German-occupied Paris in 1944. Such fateful timing for the production of a tragedy which sets the claims of idealism against those of *realpolitik* inevitably lends it resonances to which I shall revert.

I have argued in my chapter on Sophocles' play that at its outset it is possible to take a favourable view of Creon. Arrestingly, Anouilh portrays his Creon in a justifiable light throughout. Decidedly unlike Shakespeare's Prospero who lost his dukedom because of his devotion to liberal arts, Creon abandoned his cultivated pursuits when catapulted into power (4).[22] In a passionate elaboration of Sophocles' ship-of-state metaphor (lines 163 and 190), he declares that *someone* has to do the job:

Someone has to say yes. Someone has to steer the ship. It's

letting in water on all sides. It's full of crime and stupidity and suffering. The rudder's adrift. The crew won't obey orders – all they're interested in is looting the cargo. The officers are busy building a comfortable raft for themselves and cornering all the fresh water. But the mast's split, the wind's howling, the sails will soon be in shreds, and the whole lot of them will die together because they think of nothing but their own skins and their own petty concerns. And do you really think this is the moment for fine distinctions? ... No! You grab the tiller, you stand up to the mountains of water, you shout an order – and if you're attacked you shoot the first comer. The first comer! He hasn't got a name. (39–40)

Ismene can see Creon's point of view in his denial of burial to Polyneices' corpse (11) and she says that everybody in Thebes agrees with him (12). In a striking passage which turns on its head the taunt of Sophocles' Haemon that Creon is only fit to be king of an unpopulated land (739), Anouilh's ruler rejects his son's urging to ignore the people:

CREON. The mob knows already. They're all round the palace yelling. I can't turn back.
HAEMON. The mob! What does it matter? You're the master!
CREON. Under the law. Not against it. (50)

He does all in his power to avoid killing Antigone, hoping that her subversive actions can be covered up and urging her to go ahead with her marriage to Haemon and to have a son by him. (One really does need to know one's Sophocles well to appreciate fully the intertextual dialogue that Anouilh is conducting with his predecessor and to realize how radically different this attitude to Antigone makes the modern Creon.) Then, as a last resort, he tells her the truth about the contemptible nature of her brothers

Polyneices and Eteocles (41–5). The appalling picture of Polyneices is based on material from *Oedipus at Colonus*, though Anouilh has made it even blacker than Sophocles. Will she really die for someone like that?

Antigone capitulates. But then Creon throws his victory away by making it clear that the happiness he is offering her is based on lies and on closing one's eyes to dreadful truths (45). 'Don't listen,' he tells her. 'Don't listen to me when I make my next speech over Eteocles' grave. It won't be the truth. Nothing is true but what is never said.' His middle-aged cynicism revolts her. To learn it for herself would be far too high a price to pay for Creon's concept of happiness and she again determines to die. As Creon has earlier observed, 'All right – I've got the villain's part and you're cast as the heroine.' (36)

The heroine in the ring with the wrinkled, tired, flabby Creon (4 and 46) is an archetypal figure from Anouilh's early plays. As Ted Freeman[23] says, 'she is dark, small, scrawny, physically undeveloped as a woman, and ... regrets not being male'. Though she is full of the life instinct (13) and eager for sex, marriage and a son (18–20), her resolve to bury her brother means that she will inevitably die. The play makes it clear that Ismene is right when she says that Polyneices did not love her (21) but Antigone's sense of what she must do is, for the most part, quite empty of doubt. In the first movement of the great scene of confrontation her responses to Creon's unwavering fluency are simple, brief and intensely moving, the more so in that the Sophoclean model will be leading us to expect her to deliver a great bravura speech. As we have seen, her heroic determination collapses when Creon tells her the truth about her brothers; but then, after he has made the blunder of trying to displace her passionate idealism with his world-weary cynicism, Antigone becomes Antigone once more, and scornful rhetoric gushes from her lips. From p. 46 she addresses him with the contemptuous 'tu' and three times calls him a 'scullion' (cuisinier). It is true that in her desolate final scene with the clod of a guard, she loses all her confidence and the words 'I don't know any more what I'm dying for ...' are heard three times. (It may be that the self-belief of Sophocles' heroine founders in a similar way (919–26).) Her courage, however, is not broken. She leaves the stage with an effort at a smile (58). The fact that Antigone twice falters in her strength makes it clear how hard-won it is, validating rather than undermining it.

It remains true that Creon is able to rationalize his pragmatism very convincingly, while Antigone singularly fails to verbalize a justification for her idealism. It may appear glib to quote Pascal and observe that 'the heart has its reasons which reason knows nothing about', but surely the remark *does* have relevance when *realpolitik* is in conflict with an abstract ideal. A grim off-stage parallel is drawn between uncle and niece when the former replicates the latter's clawing up of earth to cover her brother's body as he digs among the stones to reach his son until his hands bleed (30–1 and 58). The ageing but still vigorous Creon (4) and the frail girl are in fact well balanced as opponents; but it is Antigone's martyrdom that will make their story live. As the Chorus exclaims, if Creon lets her die, they will all bear the scar for thousands of years (49).

A number of significant differences between Anouilh's and Sophocles' treatments have not yet been mentioned. Among them is the former's replacement of the Sophoclean chorus of 15 Theban elders with a single Prologue-Chorus, who proves to be a key element in the drama. When the play reached London in 1949, the part was acted by no less a luminary than Laurence Olivier. This role establishes at the outset an explicit metatheatrical element (see the glossary for a definition of the term and for the shadowy presence of metatheatre in Greek tragedy) as Prologue describes the real-life people gathered on stage to act the story of Antigone. I quote one particularly striking vignette:

> The pale youth alone on the other side of the room, leaning pensively against the wall, is the Messenger. He's the one who will in due course come and tell of Haemon's death. That's why he doesn't like talking and laughing with the others. He knows ... (5)

The Messenger's alienation from the rest of the actors will go on for a long time since he will be the last to appear in the play, at the very end.

Before the drama's central confrontation, in a celebrated passage beginning 'Now the spring is wound. The tale will unfold all of itself' (25),[24] Prologue-Chorus contrasts modern melodramas and thrillers, in which innocent victims can be saved from villainous oppressors, with tragedy, in which

> everybody's on a par. All innocent! It doesn't matter if one person kills and the other is killed – it's just a matter of casting ... And above all, tragedy's restful, because you know there's no lousy hope (sale espoir)[25] left. You know you're caught, caught at last like a rat in a trap, with all heaven against you. (26)

The exclamation 'All innocent!' suggests that in Anouilh's play *both* Creon *and* Antigone may be 'right', with an equal claim to innocence. And 'it's just a matter of casting' – compare 'That's how the cast-list was drawn up' on p. 11 – surely tells us that Antigone *has* to play the Antigone of the myth. Despite her unheroic moments, it is the role of the tragic heroine that she has been allocated and it is that role that she must act out: 'Her name is Antigone, and she's going to have to play her part right through to the end.' (3) Anouilh makes fine use of the Pirandellian metatheatrical concept of characters fixed in their roles.

The playwright presents his guard and his earthy colleagues in a decidedly unsympathetic light. As Freeman remarks, they are 'stupid, and alternately servile and full of bluster, keenly aware of rank and the importance of hierarchical procedures in the army. Above all they are willing to obey orders no matter how brutal ... For leisure they dream of nothing more exalted than getting away from their wives and children to spend their bonus on drinking and wenching.' They are not a good advertisement for the common man. Of course, like Anouilh's invented Nurse, they bring an element of normality into the play. However, while she is full of warmth and affection, they remain profoundly depressing. The contrast with Sophocles' Guard, who is humanized by comedy as well as by the bond he feels with the captive Antigone, is extreme. Anouilh's heroine persuades the modern guard to write down her final letter to Haemon with the bribe of a golden ring but it seems unlikely that he would have made any effort to deliver it, though he certainly pockets the ring. His lack of any sympathy with Antigone in this, her final scene makes her desolation here particularly bleak. He and his companions end the play unconcernedly playing cards, bringing to mind the soldiers at Jesus' crucifixion who cast lots for his garments (Matthew 27.35, etc.).

I must not fail to mention a few of the similarities between the modern and ancient plays since they make it clear how closely Anouilh's tragedy is based on that of the Greek master. The progress of the long day of the action from 'grey dawn' (6) is charted with equal precision in both tragedies. Again, in both Ismene tries to lay claim to a part in the burial (48–9). Anouilh's Messenger speech is a straightforward condensation of the Sophocles original. Above all, the modern dramatist follows the basic contours of the ancient plot and, even taking variations into account, one finds that the Antigone-Ismene, Antigone-Haemon and Haemon-Creon relationships are essentially replicated.

Anouilh's tragedy offers a bleak view of the human condition, with only the presence of the Page, an as yet uncorrupted boy, offering any hint of hope for the future. Here we should return to the fact that the work was written and received its first performance in occupied France. The uncomfortable truth of the matter is that the comparatively favourable presentation of Creon could reasonably be taken as an endorsement of Marshal Peìtain who had come out of retirement to take the helm of Vichy France and save the country from chaos, and / or of his Prime Minister Pierre Laval. In addition, Antigone is portrayed with too much ambivalence and too much solipsism to enable us to identify her with the heroism of the French resistance. Yet it is surely simplistic to interpret the play in a wholly political light. It is as much about how to live as how (or whether) to rule. In taking us with profound insight into both the head of Creon and the heart of Antigone, the playwright shows so great a human understanding that it is on the last count inappropriate to take sides. In response to Creons's tragedy, one might echo the words of Shakespeare's Doctor after he has witnessed Lady Macbeth's tell-tale sleepwalking: 'God, God forgive us all!' (*Macbeth*, 5.1.72) Each one of us must come to terms with the warring Antigone and Creon inside us.

Pier Paolo Pasolini's *Edipo Re*

Pasolini's 1967 film *Edipo Re* begins and ends in a twentieth-century Italian town (though the first shot of a stone signpost directs us to Thebes in Greece). Brass-band music, a war memorial. And then a boy is born. A Freudian framework for the film is established with an archetypal yet sensitive presentation of the Oedipus complex. The bonding between mother and son is wonderfully suggested as she suckles him in a green meadow surrounded by trees. Yet the beauty of the images – and Silvana Mangano's expressive performance as the mother – are lent an unsettling quality by the use of the opening of Mozart's 'Dissonance' Quartet to accompany them. The father's confused but largely hostile feelings towards his son and the tensions between them are powerfully conveyed. With strong suggestive force, the former, played by the startlingly good-looking Luciano Bartoli (who will reappear as Laius), grasps his baby son's ankles in his cradle causing him to call to his mother as the opening sequence concludes. Sexy, disturbing and profound, this is fine, richly-textured cinema. The film's concluding sequence takes us to a modern Italian city. The blind Oedipus is seen playing a pipe outside a church and then being led through an industrial landscape. Brass-band music, the war memorial of the opening, and finally the meadow with the trees and a recurrence of the 'Dissonance' Quartet. 'Life ends where it begins.' A lifetime of trauma resulting from experiences in infancy at last comes to its conclusion. This closing scene gains in power from its suggestion of the blind hero arriving at the grove of the Eumenides in *Oedipus at Colonus*.

The vast central expanse of the film moves back to a primitive society which is conveyed in a fine accumulation of detail. The Moroccan locations with their wide vistas of barren desert (in striking contrast to the green meadow of the prologue), the huge mud-built cities, and the unforgiving blue skies and the burning sun are superbly exploited; the costumes are brilliantly conceived, conveying an iron-age civilization with an impressive consistency of vision. Sophocles' narrative is unfolded chronologically, his play unpacked as a linear narrative. We actually believe the story. Oedipus' killing of Laius' escort of four soldiers is made entirely convincing in a long sequence: in a ploy familiar from the story of the Horatii and the Curiatii in Livy, the young hero runs away from the armed men, separates them and then picks them off one by one. The film's expressive imagery can be illustrated through just one of its features, its use of birds. When Oedipus is feeling the urge to travel from Corinth, they circle aimlessly, combining with Oedipus' winged hat to suggest his need to take off for Delphi; and birds mass to prey on the exposed infant and dead human flesh.

Pasolini's Oedipus is an outsider. In his travels he finds it impossible to participate in the social life of the society through which he passes, sitting to eat in front of a wall behind which a joyous wedding is being conducted with skirling music. He passes by Teiresias, who is sitting amid desert greenery (suggestive of the prologue's meadow) playing the tune from the 'Dissonance' Quartet on a pipe, and he feels totally cut off from the prophet's song of what is beyond destiny. He is not perfect: in a flashback showing him as a young man, he cheats at discus-throwing. In pious contrast, he travels holding a suppliant branch, which sets in a deplorable light Laius' rough and contemptuous bidding to him to stand aside and gives some justification for the killings that follow. However, unlike Sophocles' hero, he is not the intelligent man who solves problems – until, that is, he unravels the riddle of who he is himself. He destroys the Sphinx simply by shoving her into an abyss – no riddle here. He acts on instinct and is revealed as a neurotic by the melodramatic, silent-cinema way he has of rubbing the back of his hand against his lips as his eyes express anguish. His impulsiveness makes his anger with Teiresias, whom he ends up manhandling, entirely in character. He trusts to chance, closing his eyes at every crossroads on his journey, then spinning round and taking the route which he ends up facing. The details all add up in this convincing impersonation, which Franco Citti brings brilliantly to life.

The lead-up to the action of Sophocles' play unfolds at a leisurely pace, taking as much time as the condensed play itself. Yet it is hypnotic and riveting. Pasolini's version of the tragedy is certainly cut to the bone but it follows as much text as it reproduces very accurately, and the plague is conveyed to chilling effect. There is one puzzling moment of discontinuity in the confrontation between

Oedipus and Creon, when the former appears to be talking quietly to his wife, who is absent in their distant lofty bedroom. The succession of sex scenes between Oedipus and Jocasta communicates genuine passion. He twice calls her his love; then finally, before he knows the truth, he addresses her as mother. This instinctive access to knowledge may be a shot in the dark; but it may look forward to his comment after Jocasta's suicide that his actions were 'willed, not imposed by destiny'. That reflects the way in which Sophocles' hero takes responsibility for his self-blinding (1331–5), and no doubt looks back to the Oedipal prologue. But it does not fit in with the presentation of the hero as essentially innocent in the body of the film. It is a puzzling remark. Equally puzzling is the earlier statement on the screen, in Pasolini's trademark black on white, of Creon's interior thought: 'Oedipus refuses knowledge of his guilt and puts the blame on me and his people.' It is surely the case that the director is allowing Creon access to an implausible font of knowledge at this point.

In place of Sophocles' chorus of male elders, Pasolini presents us with a group of laughing girls who run about in each of the film's three locations, the modern town, ancient Corinth and Thebes. Their blithe giggles and their fragile femininity throw the terrors of the tragic story into grim relief. It is indeed a bleak and pessimistic retelling of the myth. And then the scene in which the shepherd who exposed Oedipus makes his true identity clear to him is played out on a lush green expanse reminiscent of the meadow of the film's opening movement. The Oedipal resonances are unmistakable.

Yet Pasolini does not plunge us entirely into a grimly deterministic world. After all, there is at least a hint of redemption in the Hermes-like figure with jingling bells in his hat – he identifies himself as 'the messenger, the news-bringer' – who leads Oedipus to the Sphinx and Teiresias to Oedipus. Played with joyous vivacity and touching sweetness by Ninetto Davoli, a Pasolini regular, he becomes Oedipus' guide in the film's final movement, the role played by Antigone in *Oedipus at Colonus*. In the Sophocles part of the film, he evinces poignant distress over his hero Oedipus' raging against Teiresias, and, when the king has blinded himself, he puts into his hands the pipe on which the modern Oedipus will play, thus initiating the final resolution. Utterly loyal and devoted, he is now called Angelo. He is indeed Oedipus' guardian angel and lends the film its one note of benediction.

Acted by a tremendous cast and directed by a master of the cinema at the height of his powers, this film still appears a masterpiece forty years on. Michael Cacoyannis' three films of Euripides are brilliant film enactments of the plays but enactments they remain rather than fully cinematic recreations. Pasolini's *Edipo Re* works as profoundly and viscerally in the cinema as a great production of Sophocles' play does in the theatre.

The Strauss / Hofmannsthal *Elektra*[26]

One opera, Auber's *La Muette de Portici*, ignited a revolution in Belgium in 1830; a ballet, the Stravinsky / Nijinsky *Rite of Spring*, provoked a riot in a Paris theatre in 1911. Simon Goldhill suggests, in an entertaining and stimulating chapter of his *Who needs Greek?: contests in the cultural history of Hellenism* (Cambridge, 2002), that the first London performances of Richard Strauss' opera *Elektra* in 1910 (the première had been in Dresden the previous year) proved a similarly explosive experience in English perceptions of classicism. Juxtaposing *Vogue*-stye photographs of Edwardian beauties in decorously lovely classical attire with two of Edyth Walker as the first London Elektra, her hair awry, her eyes protruding and her dress an off-putting black, Goldhill argues that Strauss and the poet and playwright Hugo von Hofmannsthal, whose adapted 1903 play was the opera's libretto, had presented audiences with a truly modern Elektra. In effect, they had raped and defiled the Edwardian beauties – the metaphor is mine, not Goldhill's – by creating a heroine straight out of the pages of Breuer and Freud's *Studies in Hysteria*.

I cannot myself see the London staging of *Elektra* in as revolutionary a light as Goldhill. Chaste beauties and frenzied neurotics can, after all, be around at the same time, just as in the century after the death of Sophocles the captivating loveliness of the work of the sculptor Praxiteles could coexist with the passionate, at times ugly intensity of the very different Scopas. In any case Gilbert Murray had already brought to the London stage a series of disorderly classical ladies in the London productions of his translations of Euripides in the earlier years of the new century. I also find it hard to assign to Covent Garden the central role in UK aesthetics that Goldhill allots it – though it is true that Sir Thomas Beecham, the London conductor, took the production on a national tour after the stagings in the capital. However, the Strauss / Hofmannsthal achievement was certainly a remarkable one. As they recreated Sophocles' tragedy, they revealed an unfamiliar playwright, no longer objective, pure and aloof as the Victorians had tended to find him, but intense, penetrating, disturbing and violent.

What has made the opera so durable is surely its overwhelming visceral power, what Robin Holloway refers to in a fine essay on its orchestration as its 'weight; its animal bloodiness; its screams, tearings, axings; its nightmares and processions; above all, the galumphing and colossal dance-motions with which it ends'. What I have spoken of in my chapter on the Sophocles play as an 'undertow' of disturbing elements suffers a sea-change in the opera, becoming a positive tidal wave as Strauss exploits the largest forces required by any opera in the repertory. This is, of course, a valid response of Hofmannsthal and Strauss to the violence inherent in Sophocles: the opera is awash with blood. Indeed, Hofmannsthal had wanted the blood imagery to dominate in his play and he had emphasized this by the exclusively back and red décor of the original staging. Furthermore, his Chrysothemis adds to Sophocles – rather than simply playing variations – when she describes how the murder of Aegisthus gives rise to a blood-bath of vengeance killing in the household. (Strauss decidedly underplays the violence here in his setting of the words.)

There is also the graphic underlining which conveys states of mind, most notoriously in the music for the guilt-ravaged Clytemnestra, where harmony almost breaks down (almost but not completely, according to music scholars). A self-consciously modernist, Freudian work, *Elektra* communicates the characters' warped sensibilities with startling immediacy. At the same time it mines a rich vein of tenderness to ineffably beautiful effect, above all in Elektra's aria at the start of her recognition song, composed to words that Hofmannsthal added to his original text at the composer's request.

A notable feature of the opera (preserved from Hofmannstahl's play) is that no male voice is heard until more than half way through its duration when a young servant rushes from the house to fetch Aegisthus. (Sophocles launched his tragedy with a dialogue between Orestes and his tutor.) Strauss famously loved writing for the female voice and so this initial absence of men suited him well as a composer. More significantly, the dramatic effect is to locate the action in a feminine environment, a household out of joint because of the absence of an effective paternalistic male. The tremendously authoritative Agamemnon motif that thunders forth at the start of the opera – and indeed throughout its course – repeatedly reminds us that the lawful king has been murdered.[27] The tenor Aegisthus, unmistakably a kinsman to the neurasthenic Herod of Strauss's previous opera *Salome*, is a foppish figure, the E flat clarinet which accompanies him undermining any respect.

(Hofmannsthal preserves from the Sophocles Electra's jibe about his performing his noble deeds only with women but takes it as meaning that his prowess is limited to the bedroom: the standard – and surely correct – view of the Sophocles words (302) is that they refer to the fact that he needed Clytemnestra's help – i.e. a female collaborator – to murder Agamemnon.) In a zone in which testosterone is in short supply, the baritone Orestes comes across with dignity and authority.

In this largely feminine world, the chorus consists of mainly time-serving palace servants and their Overseer. (The full-scale operatic chorus is relegated to some 27 celebratory offstage repetitions of the name Orestes in the work's ecstatic final movement.) As for Clytemnestra, Hofmannsthal has emptied her of any of the qualities that may gain our sympathy in the original. Yet so expressive is Strauss' music for her that it is hard not to feel something for this shattered, infinitely exhausted insomniac, so weighed down is she by her terrible burden of sin. Like Claudius in *Hamlet*, she calls out for light amid her spiritual darkness. Yet unlike the anguished Claudius, she feels not a hint of guilt about the evil means by which she has gained her present power and prosperity (as also in Sophocles – 647–54). And her total lack of hesitation in contemplating human sacrifice as well as her stage villain's laughter over the (false) report of Orestes' death mark her down as irredeemable.

One of the opera's most beautiful themes evokes the children of Agamemnon. It certainly plays a significant part in conveying, most movingly, Electra's profound love for her father and sounds again in accompaniment to Electra's second succession of utterances of her brother Orestes' name in the recognition scene which is the opera's emotional climax. (We have no urn scene and no recognition of the tutor to detract from its supremacy.) Yet despite her intense love she feels that she cannot embrace Orestes, so completely has her life degraded her. Her relationship with her sister Chrysothemis is also ambivalent. The latter character is powerfully drawn. She believes that she has been deprived of a normal life because of Elektra's intransigence. Her longing for children is conveyed in a passionate aria, which concludes with her assertion, 'I am a woman and I want a woman's lot.' Elektra treats her with dismissive contempt as a collaborator with the usurpers but, when she finds that she needs her to join in their murder, she wheedles her in a scene suggestive of lesbian incest. When the appalled Chrysothemis refuses to help her, Electra curses her. The emotional extremity in this scene, absent or at the most only implicit in Sophocles' play, is characteristic of Hofmannsthal's text and Strauss' music.

Hofmannsthal's adaptation is very recognizably of Sophocles' play, though the murder weapon (the axe) and the location of Agamemnon's murder (the bath) are taken from Aeschylus (the murder weapon is problematic here, however) and Euripides, while Elektra's comparison of her mother to the gods comes from the latter (*Electra* 994–5). I wonder too whether the scene in which Electra dances with her torch in welcome of Aegisthus, is a replay of Cassandra's similar antics in Euripides' *Trojan Women*. The opera's conclusion, however, in which Electra collapses dead as she dances in ecstasy, is not, of course, to be found in any of the Greek dramatists' treatments of the story. It is Hofmannsthal's innovation (though Michael Lloyd suggests that he may have been inspired by the chorus' invitation to Electra to join them in the dance after the killing of Aegisthus in Euripides' version (859–61)) – and Strauss played a vital part when he asked the playwright to give him a duet for the two sisters just before the climactic moment. At the end of this Elektra sings, 'Love kills, but who can live without love?' As he cut back Hofmannsthal's play to make it a workable libretto, Strauss eliminated most of the sexual language in which it abounds. The focus is thus on the pure, idealized love of Electra for her father and brother, love that is so intense that it kills her. We have it on good authority that 'men have died from time to time, and worms have eaten them, but not for love'. Yet such is the force of the love that Elektra feels – and so near allied is it to her hatred of her oppressors – that her *Liebestod* does convince. At this juncture of supreme joy, her emotions implode and she dies. If we may view the work in terms of operatic performance, as the soprano comes to the end of what is probably the most demanding female role in all opera, she has simply sung herself out. At all events, this conclusion with the heroine's death raises difficult questions about the positive, optimistic readings of Sophocles' play that we have outlined earlier. Surely Holloway is wrong to exclaim of the opera, 'It is glorious, but it is not Greek!' It can justly be seen as *both* glorious *and* profoundly Greek.

P.S. I hope that I may be forgiven a brief note on Richard Strauss's love affair with Greece. Writing at the age of around 81 (in summer 1945) about his first visit to Greece in 1892, he remembered that, from the moment when, 'coming from Brindisi, I saw from the deck of the Italian steamer the island of Corfu and the blue mountains of Albania, I have always been a German Greek, even to this day.

'For I can look back,' he continued, 'on artistic achievements which, like *Elektra*, *Ariadne [auf Naxos]*, *Aegyptische Helena*, *Daphne*, and *Die Liebe der Danae*, do homage to the genius of the Greek nation, and it is with pride that I sign myself with the title 'Honorary Freeman of the Isle of Naxos' bestowed on me some twenty years ago, and with pleasure that I remember the award of the Grand Cross of the Greek order of Christ.'

Seamus Heaney's *The Cure at Troy*

One of the most striking features of Seamus Heaney's 'version' of *Philoctetes* (dating from 1990) which brought Sophocles' play so movingly to the modern stage is its fidelity to the original. It occasionally expands the Greek text but never works against it; indeed it always arises naturally from it. Even though the wonderful lyrics of the chorus which launch the play's final movement are totally Heaney's invention – like the opening chorus, to which I shall return later –, they bring out and universalize what I join the poet-playwright in seeing as the essential 'message' of Sophocles' tragedy.

The specifics of the stage setting (1)[28] are very literally extrapolated from the original play but, though Sophocles is said by Aristotle to have introduced scene-painting to western theatre (*Poetics* 1449a), Heaney's naturalistic cliff-face is far more detailed than anything that might have been on show in the theatre of Dionysus in Athens. Again, an essential truthfulness to the Greek text leads to the memorable portrait of the so-called Sophoclean hero (see pp. 9–10):

> Your courage has gone wild, you're like a brute
> That can only foam at the mouth. You aren't
> Bearing up, you are bearing down. Anybody
> That ever tries to help you just gets savaged.
> You're a wounded man in terrible need of healing
> But when your friends try, all you do is snarl
> Like some animal protecting cubs. (72; cf. Sophocles,
>   1321–3)

Heaney has expanded the animal imagery in the original of this passage and he has imported the idea of healing, but the amplification is not gratuitous or distorting. As the chapter on *Philoctetes* above suggests, motifs of animals and of healing and relief from pain are woven closely into its fabric.

Other pervasive features of the original receive appropriate emphasis in Heaney's play. The theme of education finds vivid expression in the early scene in which Odysseus corrupts his pupil

Neoptolemus (6–11). The idea that Neoptolemus has been play-acting a lie is brought out effectively by Philoctetes' declaration that he has been rehearsed (53). Heaney draws out the pathos of the moments of physical contact between Neoptolemus and the physically repulsive hero with supreme sensitivity. By replicating the original play's constant evocation of the sea – Heaney's opening stage direction starts 'A sea shore. Spacious fetch of sea-light' – he provides an eloquent context for 'the great sea-change' in Philoctetes' heart (77). He also conveys an urgent awareness, which we sense in the original, that the action is set at a crucial moment, that everything depends on what happens now. Just before he meets Philoctetes, Neoptolemus exclaims, 'This is the hour of the bow!' (14)

Perhaps uniquely among twentieth-century recreators of Greek theatre, he solves the problem of the chorus for the modern theatre. A group of three women, they start the play 'boulder-still, wrapped in shawls' (1) like the Graiae of Greek mythology or Wagner's Norse Norns, then they stretch and unstiffen 'like seabirds' and their words locate them 'more or less a borderline between / The you [the audience] and the me and the it of it [the play's intractable elements]' (2). At the end of their prologue, another Heaney importation which inducts the audience into the maelstrom of emotions that lies ahead, they become lookouts and then Neoptolemus' sailors. This labile adaptability prepares us effectively for the climactic, universalizing Heaney lyrics near the close of the play. Finally the chorus leader speaks – or rather declaims ritually – as Hercules (78).

Heaney makes much of the volcano on Lemnos, a relatively unimportant feature of Sophocles' play. If it can be suggested in the background on the set, says Heaney, 'all the better', adding that 'it should not be overemphasized' (1). It coughs and splutters at the end of the prologue – 'Volcanic effects. Lurid flame-trembles, commotions and eruptions' (3) – and Philoctetes sees its crater as a location for his longed-for death on p. 45 and calls upon the volcano god on p. 55 (cf. Sophocles, 800–1 and 986–7). Then, before the climatic lyrics, it flames and rumbles, imparting a numinous aura to the poetry (76). Heaney links the volcano's flame with that of the torch with which Philoctetes set fire to Hercules' funeral pyre, thereby inheriting the latter's famous bow; and, at the moment of Hercules' appearance which leads to Philoctetes' change of mind and his rebirth, the 'full thunderclap and eruption-effects occur' (78) 'When the stone cracks open and the lava flows' (2). Philoctetes' heart melts and the play's impasse is broken. The channels are open (80).

If poetry was justly defined by Coleridge as 'the *best* words in the best order', then Heaney's fine version of *Philoctetes* certainly qualifies as such. Most of the play is written in extremely flexible and pellucid blank verse lines. One characteristically happy example comes when Neoptolemus asks Philoctetes if he can hold the bow and the hero replies in lines which convey Sophocles' meaning with impressive accuracy:

> You are allowed, son. Your natural reverence
> Gives you the right. You've brought back sunlight here.
> You've lit the world and now I'm fit to see
> A way home to my father and my friends.
> I was under the heel of enemies
> But you raised me up above them.
> You of all men have the right to hold
> Philoctetes' bow. What's mine is yours.
> You gave to me, I give to you ...
> You and you alone can tell the world
> You touched this weapon, and the reason why
> Is the reason I got it from Hercules
> In the first place: generous behaviour. (36–7; cf. Sophocles
> 662–70)

Varying the underlying iambic pulse (υ /), Neoptolemus pours out an easy, unpremeditated flow of dactyls (/ υ υ) when his true nature begins to assert itself and sets him on the honourable way ahead:

> Obviously now we could steal away with the bow.
> That would be easy. But easy and meaningless. No.
> It's to this wounded man the triumph has to be due.
> He has earned it. The oracle said it. I see it all now.
> Without him the cause will be shamed and our victory
>   hollow. (46)

Philoctetes speaks in directly communicative prose for his major onslaught on Odysseus (56–7) and his farewell to the island (80). After their iambic prologue, the lyrics of the chorus are frequently characterized by rhyme, half-rhyme and assonance. Heaney uses every weapon in the poet's armoury to communicate the range and diversity of Sophocles' dramatic voice.

We come now to the climactic lyrics of the chorus – or it may be the chorus leader – which prefigure Philoctetes' change of heart and his journey to Troy where he will be healed. They lament History's lesson that there is no hope in memorable Audenesque lines:

> The innocent in gaols
> Beat on their bars together.
> A hunger-striker's father
> Stands in the graveyard dumb.
> The police widow in veils
> Faints at the funeral home. (77)

Yet that is not necessarily the end of the story. They continue:

> But then, once in a lifetime
> The longed-for tidal wave

Of justice can rise up,
And hope and history rhyme.

So hope for a great sea-change
On the far side of revenge.
Believe that a further shore
Is reachable from here.
Believe in miracles
And cures and healing wells.

Call miracle self-healing:
The utter, self-revealing
Double-take of feeling.
If there's fire on the mountain
Or lightning and storm
And a god speaks from the sky

That means someone is hearing
The outcry and the birth-cry
Of new life at its term. (77–8)

The miracle happens. Poetry allows the god to speak (2). And then
Philoctetes 'can see / The cure at Troy' (80).[29] His restored faith in
Neoptolemus – indeed his love for him – leads the chorus to end the
play with this declaration:

    I leave
Half-ready to believe
That a crippled trust might walk

And the half-true rhyme is love. (81)

The last line, a reminiscence (I take it) of Philip Larkin,[30] concludes
the play with an eloquent poetic gesture. The 'half-true rhyme' of
'love' is conveyed in a half-rhyme (with 'leave' and 'believe'). Thus the

play ends with only partial harmony (half-harmony, as it were) and we are denied total closure. But whatever the future may hold, the god has spoken and there are some grounds for hope. At all events, his change of heart is a triumph for Philoctetes, previously so utterly intransigent, enabling him to live with uncertainty and compromise and to rejoin human society. His bonding with Neoptolemus means, to adapt Heaney's epigraph from Auden, that the crooked hero can love his crooked neighbour with his crooked heart.

The linguistic game that is being played out at the end of *The Cure at Troy* calls to mind Heaney's beliefs about poetry. There is clearly a political dimension to the play, written as it was amid the Troubles in Northern Ireland and first performed at Derry in 1990 before touring Northern Ireland and the Republic. Rightly or wrongly, I have chosen not to deal with that aspect here. Oliver Taplin feels that discussion of the play has been hijacked by this preoccupation.[31] In any case, as he observes, Heaney clearly has reservations about a reading that relates the play too specifically to Ulster: 'while there are parallels ... between the psychology and predicaments of certain characters in the play, and certain parties and conditions in Northern Ireland, the play does not exist in order to exploit them. The parallels are richly incidental rather than essential to the version.'[32] And indeed the play enters a plea for love and reconciliation as opposed to hatred and intransigence that cannot be confined to any particular local conflict. Heaney, in his first lecture as Professor of Poetry at Oxford, delivered the year before the play was produced, talked of poetry as an 'agent for proclaiming and correcting injustices' but went on to insist on the imperative 'to redress poetry *as* poetry, to set it up as its own category, an eminence established and a pressure exercised by distinctly linguistic means'.[33] Nothing could better exemplify that necessary redress than his powerful and profoundly moving version of Sophocles' play. As love for Neoptolemus fills Philoctetes' heart, it seems for a moment as if poetry may have actually succeeded in making 'hope' and 'history' rhyme.

Oedipus at Colonus and *Samson Agonistes*

John Milton's *Samson Agonistes* (1671) and Sophocles' *Oedipus at Colonus* both set before us the final day of a blind, squalidly garbed man in a foreign land at a low point of his fortunes. In both plays a series of characters visits the central figure, presenting him with challenges and temptations. In Sophocles Oedipus is offered back his home in Thebes, first by Creon (falsely), later by his son Polyneices. In Milton Samson's father Manoa and his wife Dalila tempt him with the prospect of an easy future at home. Both heroes have no difficulty in imitating the deaf adder (the reference is made explicitly at *SA* 936) which 'refuseth to hear the voice of the charmer: charm he never so wisely' (Psalm 58.4,5).

Oedipus is, of course, an old man while Samson proves to be still at the height of his powers. Yet the aged Milton, in his sixties when he wrote his tragedy, so often appears to identify with, almost to take over his protagonist that we have an inescapable sense of a long life – and one fraught with disillusion and disappointment – in this figure too.

I certainly do not want to suggest that *SA* is modelled on *OC*, though it is a curious coincidence that their length is so very similar: the former clocks in at 1758 lines, the latter (the longest surviving Greek tragedy) at 1779. In addition the three claps of thunder in *OC* (1456, 1462–3 and 1478–9) find an echo in the two off-stage sound effects of *SA* (1472, when Samson enters the theatre, and 1508–10, when he tears it down). And Samson's lines to his attendant that open the play could well have been addressed by Oedipus to Antigone:

> A little onward lend thy guiding hand
> To these dark steps, a little further on. (1–2)

The key differences in dramatic terms centre round the fact that Samson is essentially solitary, discovering himself to be fundamentally opposed to the succession of figures who visit him. It is hard, too, to see him as finding much common ground with the sententious Christian piety of the chorus, who characteristically proclaim:

> Just are the ways of God,
> And justifiable to men. (293–4)

Oedipus, on the other hand, while certainly rejecting both Creon and Polyneices, bonds movingly with Antigone, Ismene, the chorus and Theseus. Indeed, I have argued earlier that love is the keynote of his character. Yet, however distinct their journeys, the two damaged heroes arrive at a similar destination. Both feel 'rousing motions' (*OC* 1540 and *SA* 1382–3) which lead them to find true fulfilment as they die.

The very differences between the two plays point up important features in both of them. The vast gamut of the *OC* chorus' emotions, ranging from their celebratory pleasure in their native Colonus (668–719) to the bleak pessimism of 1224–38, contrasts strongly with the relentless optimism of the chorus in *SA*, unvarying save for their repulsive (Miltonic) denunciation of women (1010–60). Milton's chorus comes across as relatively superficial. Samson shoulders his responsibility for what has happened to him and comes to terms with it, while Oedipus refuses to accept that he is guilty. While the former gains strength from reacting *against* all his visitors, Oedipus finds fulfilment in part because of the devoted reciprocal relationship he has been able to build with Theseus.

Both plays, however, do traverse some similar terrain. One thinks of Oedipus' passionate hatred for his son and Samson's loathing, both physical and emotional, of his wife Dalila – 'My wife, my Traitress, let her not come near me' (*SA* 725). Both protagonists are supremely scornful, Oedipus (if scorn, as much as anger, is the register here) of Creon, Samson of the blustering *miles gloriosus* Harapha. In each of the plays the scene is set with wonderful evocative power: Antigone describes for her blind father the grove at Colonus where the nightingales sing amid the laurels, olive-trees and vines (*OC* 16–18); Samson expresses his sense of release from the foul prison air in heart-easing lines:

> but here I feel amends,
> The breath of Heav'n fresh-blowing, pure and sweet,
> With day-spring born. (*SA* 9–11 – compare also *OC* 1549–50)

Above all, of course, there is the common theme of blindness. This is so pervasively woven into the fabric of *OC* that a series of line references would overwhelm. Characteristic of the sensitivity of Sophocles' writing on this theme is l. 74 which Jebb memorably translates, 'In all that I speak there shall be sight', paraphrasing finely that 'the blind man's words will be instinct with mental vision'. And the subject summoned forth from the blind Milton some of his most visceral poetry, as in Samson's famous outburst at 80–9:

> O dark, dark, dark, amid the blaze of noon,
> Irrecoverably dark, total Eclipse
> Without all hope of day!
> O first created Beam, and thou great Word,
> Let there be light, and light was over all;
> Why am I thus bereaved thy prime decree?
> The Sun to me is dark
> And silent as the Moon,
> When she deserts the night
> Hid in her vacant interlunar cave.

Both dramatists respond with a passionate empathy to their protagonists' tragic loss of sight.

Both protagonists also find within themselves the strength to achieve victory in their deaths. We have seen how the end of OC is clouded by thoughts of what is to happen at Thebes but Oedipus' triumph remains undimmed. And the SA chorus endorse Manoa's summary of Samson's end:

> Nothing is here for tears, nothing to wail
> Or knock the breast, no weakness, no contempt,
> Dispraise, or blame, nothing but well and fair,
> And what may quiet us in a death so noble. (1721–4; cf.
>   1745–58)

If I conclude by saying that both tragedies are profoundly theatrical, this will hardly seem surprising in the case of OC, whose playwright had spent a lifetime working in the theatre. It may, however, appear an eccentric judgement in the case of SA which Milton asserted was never intended for the stage. In point of fact, the play works well in the theatre. I can vouch for this on the basis of a superb production starring Michael Redgrave at the Yvonne Arnaud Theatre in Guildford in 1965. Indeed, Milton shows a fine understanding of the workings of Greek tragedy. One very simple illustration of this is that he has grasped the convention by which all tragic messengers give the gist of what they are planning to say before they tell their story at length. More significantly, he shows a total mastery of the agonistic tendency of Greek drama. One brilliant confrontation succeeds another and the tone of each is wholly distinct. His writing for the chorus, with its fluidity of rhythm, its varying line lengths and intermittent rhymes and suggestions of rhyme, is boldly innovative and represents an extraordinarily successful attempt – and one unparalleled in its ambition – by an English poet to find an equivalent for the choral odes of Greek tragedy in the vernacular.

Above all, Milton has sought to embody in his play the Aristotelian dictum that tragedy purges through pity and fear (*Poetics* 1449b). This is in fact his epigraph to the work. Thus, when the chorus conclude the play with the observation that they have been dismissed with 'calm of mind, all passion spent', the reader will recognize that he or she too has arrived at this state of mind. And it may be that this is a state of mind that is appropriate to the contemplation of the fulfilling death of the long-suffering hero at the end of *Oedipus at Colonus* as well.

NOTES

1. The fragments with English translations are conveniently available in H. Lloyd-Jones' Loeb edition (Cambridge MA, 1996).
2. There is also an interesting discussion by Matthew Wright in a chapter in Wright (2005) entitled 'A Tragic Landscape'.
3. For those interested in seeing how the concept of the racial Other is handled in today's English studies, Michael Neill's Introduction to his 2006 Oxford World's Classics edition of *Othello* will prove a rewarding read. The valuable passage on Shakespeare's use of Leo Africanus' *Geographical Historie of Africa* (pp. 18–19) is just one element in a fascinating discussion.
4. John Gould (1996b) remarks of the *Oedipus the King* and *Antigone* choruses that they 'seem to have unusual status and to evoke unusual respect from the "heroic" characters (*OT* 911, 1223; *Ant.* 940, 988; cf. 164–9, 842)'. But he would argue that 'the tenor of their utterances ... is still not that of "civic discourse" or "democratic ideology"'. However, it is surely true that the old citizens in *Oedipus at Colonus* do strike an ideological note, suggesting proto-democratic Athens.
5. The other scores are: *OT* 61, *Phil.* and *OC* 50, *Ant.* 41, *Trach.* 37, *El.* 26.
6. L.P.E. Parker, however, is inclined to believe that the chorus remain on stage at this point (Euripides, *Alcestis* (Oxford, 2007) n.746).
7. Easterling (1997b) feels differently about Creon's decree, pointing out that, if the corpse of Polyneices had been thrown out of his country, it could have been discreetly buried there later, as Thucydides writes happened in the case of Themistocles (1.138.6). The fact that Creon cuts off this possibility, she feels, puts his action in a shocking and problematic light (pp. 26–7). In my view, this is to probe too curiously into a dramatic fact.

8. Interestingly enough, it didn't seem to worry Seamus Heaney when writing *The Burial at Thebes*, his 2004 translation of *Antigone*. Though he has slimmed the play down, this was something that he felt that he could include:

> Not for a husband, not even for a son
> Would I have broken the law.
> Another husband I could always find
> And have other sons by him if one were lost.
> But with my father gone, and my mother gone,
> Where can I find another brother, ever?

9. Further examples are given in the Oxford World's Classics edition of *Othello* by Michael Neill (2006), pp. 33–4.

10. It is interesting that hardly any stress is laid on the age of the chorus, in contrast, say, with that of *Oedipus at Colonus* or Euripides' *Heracles*. Their age only becomes important at l.1111 when they need to be old enough to recognize the Theban shepherd.

11. Burnett (1998) argues in defence of tragic avengers that 'to the Athenian way of thinking, revenge was far from being a crime that men had to abjure if they were to enter a regulated community. It was not the opposite of order, as we tend to think, but order itself in its original and vital form, the community's power to punish being only a borrowed version of each man's ingrained right to retaliate' (p. 64). Herman (2006) argues convincingly against this (pp. 128–9, 189–94), showing that Athenian litigants 'are generally at great pains to insist that they want vengeance only in the form of state-sponsored acts of repression and are not interested in private acts of violence' (pp. 190–1).

12. *Dover Beach*, 15–8.

13. Judith Affleck (2001).

14. This disturbing forward reference, which points us to the larger story into which the play's events have to be fitted, is a metatheatrical reminder to the audience that they have been watching one particular version of the myth. Such pointers are a common feature at the end of Greek tragedies.

15. The Eumenides are the 'Kindly ones', benign forces who dwell beneath the earth. A roof tile has been found at Colonus, stamped with the

words 'property of the Dread Goddesses' (Archaeological Reports published by the Hellenic Society (1989) 13).

16. 92, 287–8, 308, 459–60, 462–3, 577–8, 626–30, 634–5, 647–8, 1489–90, 1496–8, 1505–6, 1518–9, 1524–5, 1533–4 and 1552–5. The knowledge that Theseus must pass down to his heir for him to teach his heir and so thenceforth (1530–2) is the place of Oedipus' passing (1522–3). It may be the fact of the secret knowledge rather than the nature of that knowledge is what is important. I am reminded of what Alfred Hitchcock called the MacGuffin in his films. 'It is the mechanical element,' said the master, 'that usually crops up in any story. In crook stories it is most always the necklace and in spy stories it is most always the papers.' The characters care about it deeply, but what the MacGuffin is doesn't really matter. The way this secret knowledge in *OC* is given religious resonances and weight is finely analysed in Easterling (2006), pp. 140–4. In addition, there is affecting pathos in the fact that Oedipus' daughters are denied the closure of mourning at his final resting place (1724–7, 1754–63).

17. In writing about the Cambridge *Ajax*, I am indebted to the essays by L.P. Wilkinson, P.E. Easterling and P.R. Radcliffe in the programme of the centenary production (1983).

18. There was one exception to this. Janet Case of Girton College took the part of Athena in Aeschylus' *Eumenides* in 1885. Also, schoolgirls could be recruited for children's parts.

19. His two 'notable exceptions' were Macklin as Tecmessa, and Mr H.J. Cust as Teucer. 'Both actors spoke as men who felt the force and potency of sentences that fell from their lips.'

20. In a letter to E.B. Cowell (Cambridge University Library Add MS 6399.202), quoted in Pat Easterling, 'The Early Years of the Cambridge Greek Play: 1882–1912', *Classics in 19ᵗʰ and 20ᵗʰ Century Cambridge*, ed. C. Stray, CPS Supp. Vol. 24 (1999).

21. Page references are to Martin Crimp, *Cruel and Tender* (Faber & Faber, 2004).

22. Page references are to the helpful Methuen drama edition of the play (2000), with translation by Barbara Bray and commentary and notes by Ted Freeman. Quotations are from Bray's translation. Prospero: 'my library Was dukedom large enough' (*The Tempest*, 1.2.109–10). Anouilh may have been thinking of the politically quiescent Creon of

Oedipus the King.

23. See note 21.

24. Anouilh owes an important debt here to the opening of Cocteau's *The Infernal Machine* (1934). In this version of the Oedipus myth, Cocteau causes The Voice to declare in the speech that starts the play: 'Behold, spectator, ... one of the most perfect machines constructed by the infernal gods for the systematic annihilation of a mortal.'

25. 'Lousy hope' is what Creon offers Antigone. She scornfully rejects it (47).

26. In this section I have been indebted to Bryan Gilliam's *Richard Strauss' Elektra* (Oxford, 1991).

27. A recent book on Mozart, *The Cambridge Mozart Enclyclopedia*, ed. C. Eisen and S.P. Keefe (Cambridge, 2006) 146–7, suggests that this motif, which surges out in D minor, is a quotation from a melodic motif in D minor with connotations of death and violence in Mozart's *Don Giovanni.*

28. Page references are to Seamus Heaney, *The Cure at Troy: A version of Sophocles' Philoctetes* (Faber & Faber (1990)).

29. The sentence is omitted from the Faber & Faber 1990 edition but can be found in the New York edition of the same year (Farrar, Straus and Giroux). It would come on p. 79 of the former, before the final sentence of Philoctetes' speech.

30. The final lines of 'An Arundel Tomb', in which Larkin comments on the fact that the effigies of the earl and countess are holding hands:

> The stone fidelity
> They hardly meant has come to be
> Their final blazon, and to prove
> Our almost-instinct almost true:
> What will survive of us is love.

As in Heaney's play, the concluding 'love' is a half-rhyme.

31. In his excellent account of the political nature of the play in E. Hall, F. Macintosh, A. Wright (eds), *Dionysus since 69* (Oxford, 2004) 145–67.

32. M. McDonald and J.M. Walton (eds), *Amid our troubles: Irish versions of Greek Tragedy* (London, 2002) 175.

33. S. Heaney, *The Redress of Poetry* (Faber & Faber, 1995) 5–6.

SUGGESTIONS FOR
FURTHER READING
AND BIBLIOGRAPHY

Texts, commentaries and translations

All the plays are contained in two volumes in the Loeb Classical Library, edited with English translations by H. Lloyd-Jones (Cambridge MA, 1994). The monumental editions (with translations) of the Sophocles plays by Richard Jebb, which appeared between 1883 and 1896, remain unsurpassed, and in 2004 they were all reprinted by Duckworth under the general editorship of P.E. Easterling with new essays by modern scholars who look at the plays from the vantage point of the early twenty-first century. Jebb's translations have long appeared decidedly antiquated but they are impressively accurate and reponsive to the Greek. More idiomatic translations are to be found in *The Complete Greek Tragedies*, D. Grene and R. Lattimore (eds) (Chicago) and the two volumes of Sophocles in Penguin Classics. A new Penguin Classics edition of *Ajax*, *Women of Trachis*, *Electra* and *Philoctetes* in translations by David Raeburn with an introduction by P.E. Easterling will appear in 2008. A number of the plays are available in English in a lively new Cambridge series: *Antigone*, D. Franklin and J. Harrison (2003); *Ajax*, S. Dutta (2001); *Electra*, E. Dugdale (forthcoming), *Philoctetes*, J. Affleck (2001); and *Oedipus Tyrannus*, J. Affleck and I. McAuslan (2003). Also recommended is the poet Seamus Heaney's very free translation of *Antigone*, *The Burial at Thebes* (Faber & Faber, 2004).

The following plays appear in the Aris & Phillips series (Oxbow) which contain translations: *Ajax*, ed. A.F. Garvie (1998); *Antigone*, ed. A. Brown

(1987); *Electra*, ed. J. March (2001); and *Philoctetes*, ed. R.G. Ussher (1990). (Brown and March give a decidedly one-sided view of the plays they are editing.) In the Cambridge Greek and Latin Classics series, which is intended for those who know Greek, two admirable editions, *Antigone*, ed. M. Griffith (1999) and *Trachiniae*, ed. P.E. Easterling (1982), are highly recommended to Greekless readers for their introductions and notes. I have reservations about three volumes in this series, *Philoctetes*, ed. T.B.L. Webster (1970), *Electra*, ed. J.H. Kells (1973) and *Oedipus Rex* (1982, revised edition 2006).

Patrick Finglass' fine scholarly edition of *Electra* (Cambridge, 2007) can be recommended enthusiastically, though he charts the territory in a decidedly more definitive way than I feel that this unstable dramatic text allows. The edition was published too late to be included in my discussion of the play.

Books on Sophocles' plays

This is a highly selective list, limited to books in English.

The Duckworth Companions to Greek and Roman Tragedy offer accessible new introductions to the ancient plays. Of those that have so far appeared, J. Hesk's *Sophocles: Ajax* (2003) and M. Lloyd's *Sophocles: Electra* (2005) are particularly helpful. Also valuable are B. Levett's *Sophocles: Women of Trachis* (2004) and H.M. Roisman's *Sophocles: Philoctetes* (2005).

Further recommendable books, in addition to those mentioned in Chapter 1 (details in bibliography), are:

Garvie, A.F. (2005) *The Plays of Sophocles* (Bristol Classical Press) – an excellent set of brief studies.

Jones, John (1962) *On Aristotle and Greek tragedy* (Chatto & Windus) – a book that still stands up well as a discussion of the application of Aristotle's *Poetics* to Greek tragedy.

Segal, Charles (1995) *Sophocles' Tragic World: Divinity, Nature, Society* (Cambridge MA) – a structuralist reading.

Winnington-Ingram, R.P. (1980) *Sophocles: An Interpretation* (Cambridge) – the classic English book on the plays.

Bibliography

Bowra, C.M. (1944) *Sophoclean Tragedy* (Oxford).

Breuer, Joseph and Sigmund Freud (2004) *Studies in Hysteria*, trans. Nicola Lockhurst (Penguin).

Burkert, Walter (1985) *Greek Religion: Archaic and Classical*, tr. John Raffan (Basil Blackwell).

Burnett, Anne Pippin (1998) *Revenge in Attic and Later Tragedy* (California).

Carter, David (2007) *The Politics of Greek Tragedy* (Bristol Phoenix Press). Recommended.

Csapo, Eric and William J. Slater (1994) *The Context of Ancient Drama* (Ann Arbor).

Devereux, George (1973) 'The Self-Blinding of Oidipous in Sophokles: *Oidipous Tyrannos*', *Journal of Hellenic Studies* 93, 36–49.

Dodds, E.R. (1973) 'On misunderstanding the *Oedipus Rex*', in *The Ancient Concept of Progress and Other Essays* (Oxford).

Dugdale, Eric (2008) *Greek Tragedy in Context* (Cambridge).

Easterling, P.E. (1993) 'Tragedy and ritual', in R. Scodel (ed.), *Theatre and Society in the Classical World* (Ann Arbor).

Easterling, P.E. (ed.) (1997a) *The Cambridge Companion to Greek Tragedy* (Cambridge) – a good collection of essays reflecting modern preoccupations in the study of tragedy.

Easterling, P.E. (1997b) 'Constructing the Heroic', in Pelling (1997).

Easterling, P.E. (2006) 'The death of Oedipus and what happened next', in D. Cairns and V. Liapis (eds), *Dionysalexandros: Essays on Aeschylus and his fellow tragedians in honour of Alexander F. Garvie* (Classical Press of Wales).

Eyre, Richard (2002) *National Service: diary of a decade* (Bloomsbury), 340–1.

Foley, Helene (2001) *Female Acts in Greek Tragedy* (Princeton).

Freud, Sigmund (1971) *The Interpretation of Dreams* (*Traumdeutung*), trans. and ed. James Strachey (Allen and Unwin).

Goldhill, Simon (1987) 'The Great Dionysia and Civic Ideology', *Journal of Hellenic Studies* 107, most conveniently available in Winkler and Zeitlin (eds) (1990).

Goldhill, Simon (1997) 'Modern critical approaches to Greek tragedy', in P.E. Easterling (ed.) (1997a).

Goldhill, Simon (2002) *Who needs Greek?: contests in the cultural history of Hellenism* (Cambridge).

Gould, John (1988) 'The Language of Oedipus', in H. Bloom (ed.), *Sophocles' Oedipus Rex* (New Haven), most conveniently available in Gould (2001).

Gould, John (1996a), under Sophocles in *The Oxford Classical Dictionary*, third edition (Oxford, 1996).

Gould, John (1996b) 'Tragedy and Collective Experience', in M.S. Silk (ed.), *Tragedy and the Tragic: Greek Theatre and Beyond* (Oxford), most conveniently available in Gould (2001).

Gould, John (2001) *Myth, Ritual Memory, and Exchange: Essays in Greek Literature and Culture* (Oxford).

Green, Richard and Eric Handley (1995) *Images of the Greek Theatre* (British Museum).

Hall, Edith (1989) *Inventing the Barbarian* (Oxford).

Hall, Edith and Fiona Macintosh (2005) *Greek Tragedy and the British Theatre 1660–1914* (Oxford).

Hall, Edith (2006) *The theatrical cast of Athens: Interactions between Ancient Greek Drama and Society* (Oxford). (See especially 'Recasting the barbarian'.)

Hardwick, Lorna (2003) *Reception Studies*, Greece and Rome New Surveys in the Classics 33 (Oxford).

Herman, Gabriel (2006) *Morality and Behaviour in Democratic Athens: a social history* (Cambridge).

Holloway, Robin (2003) *On Music: Essays and Diversions, 1963–2003* (Claridge Press).

Knox, Bernard (1964) *The Heroic Temper* (California and Cambridge).

Knox, Bernard (1984) introduction to *Oedipus the King* in *The Three Theban Plays*, trans. R. Fagles (Penguin Classics). Knox' argument that Oedipus is an embodiment of the Athenian spirit is worked out at length in his *Oedipus at Thebes: Sophocles' tragic hero and his time* (Yale, 1957).

Ley, Graham (2007) *The Theatricality of Greek Tragedy: playing space and chorus* (Chicago).

McClure, Laura (1999) *Spoken Like a Woman* (Princeton).

McDonald, Marianne and J. Michael Walton (eds) (2007) *The Cambridge Companion to Greek and Roman Theatre* (Cambridge). This book appeared too late for inclusion in the body of my text. I was delighted to see McDonald's appreciative discussion of Pasolini's film *Edipo Re* (pp. 320–3).

Morwood, James (2002) *The Plays of Euripides* (Bristol Classical Press).

Mossman, Judith (2001) 'Women's Speech in Greek Tragedy: The case of Electra and Clytemnestra in Euripides' *Electra*', *Classical Quarterly* 51.2.

Murray, Gilbert (trans.) (1905) *The Electra of Euripides* (George Allen) p. vi.

Murray, Gilbert (2005) *Gilbert Murray's Euripides*, introduction by James Morwood (Bristol Phoenix Press).

Parker, Robert (1999) 'Through a Glass Darkly: Sophocles and the Divine', in J. Griffin (ed.), *Sophocles Revisited* (Oxford).

Parker, Robert (2005) *Polytheism and Society at Athens* (Oxford).

Pelling, Christopher (ed.) (1997) *Greek Tragedy and the Historian* (Oxford).

Rehm, Rush (2002) *The Play of Space: spatial transformation in Greek tragedy* (Princeton).

Rhodes, P.J. (2003) 'Nothing to do with democracy: Athenian drama and the *polis*', *Journal of Hellenic Studies* 123.

Schlegel, A.W. von (1840) *A Course of Lectures on Dramatic Art and Literature*, trans. J. Black (London).

Scullion, Scott (1994) *Three Studies in Athenian Dramaturgy* (Teubner).

Seaford, Richard (2000) 'The social function of Attic tragedy: a response to Jasper Griffin', *Classical Quarterly* 50.

Segal, Charles (1986) *Interpreting Greek Tragedy: Myth, Poetry, Text* (Cornell), 11.5 and 11.7.

Sommerstein, A., S. Halliwell, J. Henderson and B. Zimmermann (eds) (1993) *Tragedy, Comedy and the Polis* (Bari).

Sourvinou-Inwood, Christiane (2003) *Tragedy and Athenian Religion* (Lanham, MD).

Storey, Ian C. and Arlene Allan (2005) *A Guide to Ancient Greek Drama* (Basil Blackwell).

Strauss, Richard (1953) *Recollections and Reflections*, ed. Willi Schuh, trans. L.J. Lawrence (Boosey & Hawkes).

Taplin, Oliver (1977) *The Stagecraft of Aeschylus* (Oxford).

Taplin, Oliver (1978) *Greek Tragedy in Action* (Routledge).

Taplin, Oliver (1987) 'The mapping of Sophocles' *Philoctetes*', *British Institute of Classical Studies* 34.

Taplin, Oliver (1999) 'Spreading the word through performance', in S. Goldhill, R. Osborne (eds), *Performance Culture and Athenian Democracy* (Cambridge).

Vernant, Jean-Pierre, 'Ambiguity and Reversal: On the Enigmatic Structure of *Oedipus Rex*', in E. Segal (ed.), *Oxford Readings in Greek Tragedy* (Oxford, 1983). Vernant's essay dates from 1977–78.

Waldock, A.J.A. (1951) *Sophocles the Dramatist* (Cambridge).

Wiles, David (1991) *The Masks of Menander* (Cambridge).

Wiles, David (1997) *Tragedy in Athens: performance space and theatrical meaning* (Cambridge).

Winkler, J.J. (1990) 'The Ephebes' Song: Tragoidia and Polis', in Winkler and Zeitlin (eds). Winkler's argument that the dance-song of the chorus is the ephebes' song will leave many unpersuaded, but he gives a lot of information about ephebes.

Winkler, J.J. and F.I. Zeitlin (eds) (1990) *Nothing to do with Dionysos? Athenian Drama in its Social Context* (Princeton).

Wright, Matthew (2005) *Euripides' Escape-Tragedies: A Study of* Helen, Andromeda *and* Iphigenia among the Taurians (Oxford).

Zeitlin, Froma (1990) 'Thebes: Theater of Self and Society in Athenian Drama', in Winkler and Zeitlin (eds).

GLOSSARY

aporia – a situation in which a text's self-contradictory meanings cannot be resolved.

Aristotle – The great Greek philosopher, who lived from 384 to 322 BC, i.e. in the century after Aeschylus, Sophocles and Euripides, wrote the *Poetics*, a treatise on Greek tragedy. In one key passage he asserts that tragedy purges those who experience it by making them experience pity and fear (1449b). In another he says that two ingredients of tragedy, recognition (*anagnōrisis*) and reversal (*peripeteia*), work best when they coincide with each other, 'as in *Oedipus [the King]*' (1452a).

deus ex machina – a god who appears aloft at the end of a number of tragedies and solves the problems of the play.

Dionysia – the dramatic festival of Dionysus at Athens.

ekkyklēma – a wheeled platform which was rolled out from the doors of the stage building in order to display a *tableau* of what had happened in the house.

ephebe – a young Athenian man undergoing military training.

hamartiā – In his Loeb edition of Aristotle's *Poetics* (Cambridge MA, 1995), Stephen Halliwell sums up Aristotle's use of the word thus: it 'embraces all the ways in which human vulnerability, at its extremes, exposes itself not through sheer, arbitrary misfortune (something inconsistent with the intelligible plot structure which Aristotle requires of a good play), but through the erring involvement of tragic figures in their own sufferings'.

hubris – the Greek word for 'insolence', 'affront' and 'assault and battery', it is sometimes used in tragedy of behaviour that refuses to be contained within the human sphere and trespasses on the territory of the gods.

iambic rhythm – the basic pulse of the verse of the non-choral parts of Greek tragedy, ʊ /: 'To be or not to be ...'

metatheatre – a word that refers to those instances where a play draws attention to its own status as a work of theatre, as when Jaques in *As You Like It* says, 'All the world's a stage ...' No Greek tragedy does this explicitly but the idea of the play certainly appears to be invoked at times. In Sophocles this is perhaps especially clear in *Electra*, in which Orestes stages the fictional play that will trap Clytemnestra.

orchēstra – the 'dancing place', the area between the stage building and the audience where the chorus performed.

scholion – an ancient scholar's marginal note in the manuscript of a classical author.

INDEX